Why Science Fair Sucks
And
How You Can Save It

a survival manual for science teachers

Adam Shopis

for Tracy, Laryssa and Liz

Who Should Read This Book

I wrote this book entirely from my perspective as a seventh grade science teacher. So my thinking about the type of student and the level of complexity revolves around the middle school age range. Furthermore, the lesson outlines, rubrics, and other items in the appendix represent artifacts from my seventh grade classroom.

However, the book definitely has applicability beyond the middle school grades. After all, Science Fair sucks no matter what grade you teach. Moreover, the basic premise we used to save Science Fair in my grade can be applied to elementary and high school grades alike.

I recommend you read the book and use what works for you. Every teacher works in different circumstances. Some teachers' schedules may not allow for complete application of the process described in the book. Moreover, the amount of team level work might not be possible given the organizational structure of some schools. However, once again, the basic premise used to transform Science Fair from a fiasco in which little education takes place into a rigorous learning experience can be applied, at its core, in most any classroom.

Why Science Fair Sucks
And
How You Can Save It

a survival manual for science teachers

Adam Shopis

1. Why Science Fair Sucks

Preamble

Science Fair came into my teaching life on my very first day as a teacher. Three weeks before the start of that first year of school, I'd been called in for a planning session. I sat around a table with other teachers brainstorming ideas for the brand new sixth grade that was being added to the school's original k-5 span. Chart paper with diagrams, word webs, and sticky notes hung on the walls like ancient peeling wallpaper. They outlined ways to make the transition to a middle school program, and contained ideas for new types of learning students could do now that they advanced beyond their elementary years.

We had a large task and my principal had assembled an experienced team to confront it. The team consisted mostly of seasoned teachers chosen from the current school staff plus me: the new science guy. My background in informal science education at a science museum helped a bit, but didn't prepare me for the huge work of formal teaching (not to mention building a science program from the ground up). So, when it came my turn to stand up and offer ideas for the new science program I said, "How about a science fair?"

Those words would come back to haunt me in the form of hours and years of tedious, frustrating, unsuccessful work added to an already challenging curriculum. However, it seemed simple at the time. What's the big deal? Pick a question. Test it out. Put the results on a tri-fold poster board. A pretty simple assignment, right?

I heard that. Yes, I heard you chuckling at that last statement. In the twelve years since that first day of planning, I've come to realize exactly what you now know. According to Global Language Monitor, there are 1,013,913 words in the English language. Any one of them would be a more apt description for Science Fair than the word "simple."

Why it's not "simple"

Let's get a definition of Science Fair going. For me, Science Fair consists of a series of pieces. First, there's the project. For Science Fair, students conduct an independent, at-home, scientific experiment. The experiment tasks the students with putting together many steps including, stating a testable question, researching the question, making a hypothesis, designing an investigation (an experimental procedure), conducting their experiment and gathering data, analyzing and organizing the data (usually as graphs/tables), drawing a conclusion, writing it all up in a lab report, and finally creating a visual display board that summarizes their whole experiment.

The next part of the Science Fair experience happens on the day of the fair itself. On this day students "dress for success," set up their tri-fold boards and wait while judges make their way through all the projects. Finally, the science staff announces the winners. For many, that concludes Science Fair. In some districts, the winners may go on to compete at a higher district or state level.

That whole experience from giving the assignment, to the back and forth of rough drafts/feedback/final drafts of each piece to presentation day is what I'm calling "Science Fair." *Phew*. It's a lot for us science teachers to wrap our minds around. Imagine the reactions of the kids!

The first time around, many teachers (myself included), write up all the steps in a directions pack, give out the assignment, and wait to see what comes back. Does this sound familiar? My first year I allotted many weeks for students to complete the assignment, thinking they'd work on it gradually over time. I'm not sure why I expected this. All I needed to do was to think back on my own school project experiences to realize that no one would start until a few days before it was due.

This became apparent as I checked in with students about the project along the way. Not only did most put it off, but the few who had shown initiative and got their project rolling had serious flaws in virtually every aspect of their experiment. They had devised untestable questions, with inappropriate hypotheses, and irrelevant procedures unlikely to get them any data at all not to mention relevant data. As I worked with individual students, I began to see that the Science Fair train sped along the tracks at ridiculous speed heading exactly for a giant cliff. I wanted to hit the breaks or slow down, but that option did not exist. School schedules had been set, rooms had been booked, and judges had put in for time off from their real jobs to come in for fair day.

The inevitable happened. The train, heading for a cliff at incredible speed, did exactly what all things do when confronted with gravity and altitude. It plummeted to a fiery wreck of baking soda volcanoes, moldy bread, and unanswered (unanswerable) questions.

That year (and just about every year since then) my efforts in Science Fair represented the hardest work I'd ever done with the worst payoff. However, a weird thing happened the next day, after that first fair. I received hearty congratulations from many colleagues and my principal. It almost made me feel that I had accomplished something. Almost. I had read all the reports and assessed all the tri-fold boards. I had seen the train wreck. I knew the reality. Does this sound familiar? Have you conducted the Science Fair train off the cliff...more than once? I definitely have.

Just to be clear, there were a handful of excellent projects. Some of the students received significant support at home and had a lot of help puzzling through the many steps of the assignment. These kids represented the extreme minority. Furthermore, by the time Science Fair rolls around, I already had an idea of which kids received such support at home. In an urban setting such as where I teach, significant at-home involvement occurs much less frequently than we would all hope. So, each year I could pretty much predict which students would win the Science Fair before I even gave the assignment. Obviously, this raises serious equity issues. Fear not, my ultimate solution goes a long way to solve this problem.

What is it about Science Fair that makes it such a train wreck year after year? After all students do projects in most of their other classes all the time. They write papers on novels in Language Arts. They research historical figures in social studies. They measure and redesign the school playground in math. Those trains seem to arrive safely at their designated stations. Why does the science train always seem to veer uncontrollably toward the tallest cliff on the line?

Let's look at the first thing students must do for their Science Fair project: pick a question. Each student receives the task of choosing a question that he or she will answer by doing an experiment. We encourage them to choose a question on a topic that interests them. For me, the array of questions that they end up choosing has usually indicated a severe need for support. However, it's not support that can be delivered like a typical lesson to the whole class. Indeed, because all students have chosen their own questions on a variety of topics, representing different levels of complexity, each student requires specific individual support. A few comments on a passed back sheet of paper will not do the trick. They need real planning, formative assessing, and scaffolding. They need teaching...not just feedback. The level of individuation goes beyond mere differentiated instruction. Differentiated instruction occurs when students are grappling with the same content and have different needs. For Science Fair, because of the level of unique teaching required, the correct model for doing this is individual tutoring, not whole class teaching. This actually occurs with those few students who have significant support at home. For most, the feedback we give them will not do the trick. They never revise their questions to a form that can lead to a successful experiment.

In short, the task of assigning a question that can be tested on a topic of their choosing is too big. It's not really an assignment. It's twenty-eight different assignments per class. Each student gets a different assignment and requires a unique set of lessons tailored exactly to them to support their progress. Since the whole project will spring from this question, it's pretty much doomed from the start.

Then students move on to doing background research. I require students to do library or internet research on their topic. The idea is that by doing this research they'll gain knowledge on their topic so that they can make a more informed hypothesis.

Here's what I learned my first year: students don't know how to do research. What came back were random "facts" they found from places like "Yahoo Answers," and "eHow.com." Much of their research was irrelevant and all of it was poorly cited. Many students cited "Google.com" as a source. *Ugh*. It became very clear to me that first year, that students would not complete successful background research without a series of dedicated lessons on the topic. However, the train had left the station and picked up more speed each day. I tried to help with as much individual feedback as possible. This train, though, had a lot of inertia.

Something like this repeats for every step of the project. After a couple years doing this, the pattern became clear. Students complete a step in the process. I see the amount of individual support needed. I give as much as I can. It's not nearly enough. Train rolls off the cliff. "Congratulations, Mr. Shopis, another great Science Fair." *Seriously*?

Perhaps this pattern looks familiar to you. It's not like we don't try to get that train to its station. We work many, many hours on providing support and feedback. It's just never enough.

The consequences are severe. We and our students spend huge amounts of time on this endeavor and we get two results: bad scientific process and bad scientific content. Their experiences with designing an experiment do not prepare them for doing it again the next year. Their new teacher will basically start from scratch. Moreover, no one cares which bar of soap floats and which one sinks. That's irrelevant, non-standards based content. Everybody loses. Yet we always get that congratulations and we do it again: year after year.

There is an answer, though. It's coming up soon enough. Now that I've broken down why Science Fair fails a bit, I'm going to delve into what we often try to do to fix it, why that also fails, and how to reorganize to make it all work.

2. Why Our Solutions Suck

Solution 1: The Science Fair Packet

If you've worked as a teacher for more than five years, you represent about half of all the teachers who started when you did. The work seemed insurmountable, but you plowed through it one lesson plan, one stack of exams, one high stakes test at a time. You persevered. You are one of the few who didn't give up and go to business school because the job of educating children seemed impossible. Of course you applied this tenacity to Science Fair, just like you did to every other challenge you faced.

Why, even after years of working harder to make Science Fair better, does it still suck? Let's look at some of the solutions that I applied to the problem. In my second and third year of teaching, I realized that students needed way more support than I had provided to conclude a successful Science Fair project. I saw that students hadn't really wrapped their minds around the whole endeavor. I needed to create a much more explicitly stated assignment with clear goals and complete directions for reaching them.

So, each of those years I strove to give them a more thoroughly defined assignment with better directions. I broke down the assignment into more discrete chunks. Moreover, I wrote elaborate and detailed descriptions for each part or the assignment. The instructions included a section for the question, a section for the hypothesis, procedure, all the way to how to put together the final report and Science Fair board. Each section had a description that varied in length from one paragraph to more than a page. I tried to think of every question students might have and include information about it in the directions.

I also provided ample information about how I would assess the project. I included a rubric for each section of the project as well as an overall rubric. I explicitly stated my expectation for each section and outlined what students would need to do to meet that expectation.

In addition, I included timelines. The packet had a timeline for several of the individual sections and for the project as a whole. I imagined that students could use the timelines to pace themselves so they could digest and complete the chunks of the project gradually over time. These timelines also included checklists so students could keep track of what they'd done and what they still had to do.

Moreover, I included links to web resources. I had done thorough searches of Science Fair resources on the internet. Some sources had breakdowns of different parts of the project. Some included links to exemplar Science Fair projects. Some web sites provided more explanation for the different parts of the project. A few even had tutorial videos. All of these links and descriptions of what students would find at each one were outlined in the directions packet.

The result: a packet of directions with ever-increasing thickness. If I couldn't give them actual, personal, one-on-one tutoring, then perhaps I could think of all the support I would give them and include it in a written document. They could read it, and refer to it all throughout their project. What could go wrong? *Wink.*

To say the projects that resulted did not represent a significant improvement sugarcoats it. In some ways giving a giant packet of elaborate directions made no difference or made it worse. Too many directions, with too many parts and too many words all turn into noise at some point. It was almost like handing students a thick science textbook and saying "Here you go. Learn." No teacher would ever teach that way because no student learns that way. Students cannot teach a whole science curriculum to themselves. A few students muddled through the packet and only came back with more questions than in previous years. The giant packet with explanations, rubrics, and timetables flopped. It also wasted huge amounts of paper and I became persona non grata in the copy room as teachers lined up waiting for my double sided, stapled giant packets to finish.

In subsequent years, I tried breaking the packet apart. I thought giving them the directions one chunk at a time might make it seem more doable. This improved things a little but did not address the central problem: they needed the individual support. Super elaborate written directions could not replace that, even in tiny chunks. Moreover, this piecemeal approach had the effect of extending the timeline and threatening completion by Science Fair day.

Solution 2: Bring It Into the Classroom

So, if the giant packet of instructions to be completed at home didn't work, the next logical step is to do more work in class. This would allow some group instruction on writing testable questions, and designing procedures. So, when they gave it a stab at home, it would not be a stab in the dark.

I began with a small number of lessons around writing testable questions. I tried to keep the number of lessons to a bare minimum. After all, I was also teaching a unit on Weather during this time. Every day I spent on Science Fair meant subtracting a lesson from the Weather Unit. I taught the lessons, assessed student work, and gave as much feedback as possible.

This seemed like a reasonable solution. Science Fair is a big project. Students would need instruction on it. Spending a little class time on Science Fair seemed warranted and would result in better projects. Students would get more out of the endeavor. Problem solved, right?

Here's how it went. The first year I did this, I realized that I hadn't spent NEARLY enough in-class time on it. The improvements I saw in students' projects were miniscule. They needed much more instruction than the few lessons I had devised. By the time the Science Fair day rolled around the projects looked essentially the same. Train wreck. "Congratulations on another great Science Fair, Mr. Shopis."

The next year I determined to do better. I carved out more time from the Weather unit. I wedged in a few more lessons. We did more drafting and revising. Then when Science Fair day came...wait for it...train wreck. "Congratulations, Mr. Shopis."

I began to despair. I did not want to set my students up for failure as I clearly had done. I would do better next year. I think you see where this approach is going. Each year I devoted more and more class time to Science Fair. The results were very tiny improvements in Science Fair projects and student learning. I enlisted the help of the other teachers on my team. At first one lesson's worth of time. This expanded to days and weeks. Science Fair threatened to take over everything. It was like a gas. It would expand to fill any container I tried to put it in...no matter the size. The integrity of the Weather unit began to crack and shatter. The teaching of English, history, and math became compromised as all the classrooms became cluttered with tri-fold boards, cut out construction paper, glue sticks, and glitter. That little idea I had put forth on my first day as a teacher had become a monster that threatened to eat my classroom, maybe my school if we let it.

3. Why Science Fair Sucks for Kids

Science Fair sucks for kids, even with my "solutions." First and foremost, it sucks because they don't learn anything. Each year I worked closely with the teacher who taught seventh and eighth grade science. Even though she taught the exact same kids I had taught the year before, she had to start teaching Science Fair all over again...beginning with creating testable questions. When she got the same kids again in eighth grade, the same pattern persisted. The kids remembered doing Science Fair. They may even remember which brands of soap sink and which float. However, they had not advanced in their scientific thinking and the scientific method.

Tragically, this renders moot the whole purpose of Science Fair. Science Fair is supposed to give kids experiences in the process of science. My current supervisor has a T-shirt hanging on her door that says "Science Is a Verb." Science Fair is supposed to be an experience where students get to do science, not just gain understanding of scientific content. Science Fair failed to teach them science process.

Additionally, the students learned irrelevant or even erroneous content. Once again, who really cares which brands of soap float and which sink? The vast majority of topics did not connect to standards assessed in our state high stakes test. Moreover, students' nascent expertise on writing experimental procedures often would not provide them with anything like reliable data. So students would proudly declare that adding orange juice to soil helped their lima beans grow. Yikes.

The bottom line for kids is that Science Fair teaches bad process and bad content. The process part is taught again and again to seeming no avail. The content at best does not derive from state standards and at worst is just wrong! It's a one-two punch leaving both the Teacher and Student knocked out. Yet, each year after rising off the mat...

"Congratulations, Mr. Shopis." Eventually, I started feeling like the fictional character Inigo Montoya from *The Princess Bride*. "You keep on using that word. I do not think it means what you think it means."

Science fair also sucks for kids because not only do they learn very little from it, but it compromises the part of science class where they do learn: the normal day-by-day curriculum. Each year I kept spending more and more class time on Science Fair. School was (and is) a zero sum game. I had a total of 180 days to deliver instruction on an array of state standards. Each day I spent on Science Fair subtracted one from that total number. As I tried to improve Science Fair each year, the number dwindled further and further.

The result: I taught less content each year. I began to evaluate which pieces of the curriculum could go and which couldn't. Each year I removed a girder here, a rivet there from the scaffolding that supported their content knowledge. The increasing shakiness of the final structure became obvious very quickly. It showed up in classwork, quizzes, tests, and other assessments. Moreover, our state test results inched downward. (By the way, when we fixed Science Fair, we fixed this problem, too. More on that later.)

In addition to teaching them little and compromising the rest of the curriculum, Science Fair turned kids off to science. This represented a severe irony because part of the reasoning behind the project was to give students an opportunity to pursue something they were personally interested it. It was supposed to be the one time of the year where they became super-engaged because it was their own topic!

The opposite was true. Even though I spent ever-increasing amounts of class time on Science Fair, it was never enough. I could never provide the students with the tutoring model of teaching required by this type of assignment. Students became lost, frustrated, resigned to failure. They hated Science Fair. Students who were marginally interested in science, turned away from it completely. Other students decided they only liked science when they watched it on the Discovery Channel but doing it themselves sucked. The few students who did learn a lot from the project and whose curiosity was fed rather than squashed were, predictably, the kids who had a lot of support at home. These kids got the tutoring they needed.

Science Fair has created a whole additional level of suck for students and even for the future of our country. Science Fair discouraged kids from taking more science courses. I now teach in a school that spans grades seven through twelve. So I have the opportunity to follow students over six years until they go to college. Science Fair discouraged kids from taking more science on two levels. First, it convinced them that they didn't like science. "If this is science, then no thank you," the thinking goes. This represents a severe shame bordering on crime. As Carl Sagan said, "Every kid starts out as a natural-born scientist, and then we beat it out of them. A few trickle through the system with their wonder and enthusiasm for science intact." Science Fair was the bat used in the beating.

Additionally, the students who did manage to "trickle through" to the upper grades sometimes avoided taking elective science classes. Students found the cool "Biomedical Research" class offered to Juniors and Seniors an interesting offering. Guess what question they wondered about when contemplating taking this new class? "Do I have to do Science Fair?"

The U.S. Department of Commerce indicates that over the past decade jobs in Science and Technology have outpaced job growth in other sectors by three-to-one and pay twenty-six percent more. Moreover, this job growth in Science and Technology will double in the next decade.[1] We need to stop turning kids off to science and start encouraging them to take more science. Giving them a shot at a career in science provides them with a path to the middle class. This is especially important for poorer kids. Moreover, if we don't train the next generation of scientists in this country, another country will. America will become less competitive, less innovative and less growth oriented in the future. It's kind of amazing how much suck can come from one little assignment. "Congratulations, Mr. Shopis."

The negative effect on students represents the most troubling aspect of Science Fair. However, Science Fair sucks for teachers as well.

Spending more and more time working through Science Fair meant less and less time teaching my regular curriculum. Through the regular curriculum, I provided students with daily inquiry experiences that brought them up to rigorous state standards. However, with Science Fair absorbing more and more of my class time, I accomplished this less and less every year. I needed more time on curriculum, not less.

I also got an increasing annual sense of bashing my head against the wall. Teachers who make it past their fifth year do not fear long, grueling hours of work. However, we despair when that work accomplishes little. I look for ways to work "smarter not harder." Putting more and more work into Science Fair resulted in the opposite.

Albert Einstein once said the definition of insanity was "doing the same thing over and over again and expecting different results." Fellow science teacher, I have developed a hypothesis about us: We're all nuts. Each year we plunge head first into this endeavor called Science Fair and hope it will work this time. It doesn't. It never will…at least not if we keep doing the same thing . The solution I'll offer you in this book embraces the following radical proposition: do it differently.

---

[1] U.S. Department of Commerce. STEM: Good Jobs Now and For the Future. By David Langdon, George McKittrick, David Beede, Beethika Khan, and Mark Doms. Available at: http://www.esa.doc.gov/sites/default/files/reports/documents/stemfinaljuly14_1.pdf

4. Why We Do Science Fair Anyway

"We must address the low standing of American test scores amongst industrialized nations in math and science, the very subjects most likely to affect our future competitiveness." - **George W. Bush**

"One of the things that I've been focused on as President is how we create an all-hands-on-deck approach to science, technology, engineering, and math… We need to make this a priority to train an army of new teachers in these subject areas, and to make sure that all of us as a country are lifting up these subjects for the respect that they deserve" - **Barack Obama**

"I don't think we are at all in denial about the fact that our science scores and performance are nowhere close to where we want them to be" - **Carol Johnson, former Superintendent of Schools, Boston.**

Leaders on all levels have expressed the need to increase student success in science in this country. No one would argue otherwise. For some reason, though, this sentiment doesn't translate in the classroom like it did when math and English needed reform.

When "No Child Left Behind" and its high stakes tests came to town, radical changes came to classrooms throughout my district. Additional district administrators were hired. New texts books were ordered. Huge amounts of teacher training was conducted. Coaches were hired and placed in schools. New and better curricula were reviewed and adopted. Data analysis systems and training were purchased. In short, tons of money was invested in aligning to and achieving new state standards. NCLB tested only English and math at first so schools focused there.

However, when it's time to ramp up our efforts in science, instead of a similar all-out effort to reform teaching and learning we get...Science Fair. What the...? Where are the coaches, the materials, the teacher training, data analysis? Heck, students in my district only get assessed in Science once in Elementary School, once in Middle School and once in High School! Not that I possess a great love for high stakes testing, but it shows where priorities lie. (Hint: It's not with science education.)

So why is this happening? Why, when everyone from presidents on down publicly recognize the need for improvement in science, do we still do Science Fair? Why do we insist on engaging in an activity that sucks for kids and sucks for teachers and, ultimately, sucks for the whole country?

One reason: it's a no cost, highly visible way to appear to make an investment in science. No software gets purchased. No training gets organized. No new curriculum gets tested and adopted. No coaches get placed in schools. No labs get updated. No data gets crunched. In short: no money gets spent. However, the community sees the tri-fold boards and students dressed in their best cloths. It looks like something big is happening. The newspapers cover it. It's sexy and cheap. Any administrator can get behind that!

A few students go on to compete at higher levels of Science Fair. These students often get celebrated in the school and town they're from. Sometimes they appear in a feature article in the local paper. My second year teaching, one of my students went on to place first in the statewide Science Fair. I was told this was a first in over a decade for my city. The district newspaper wrote an article on her. I got way more recognition for that than for the year my students outperformed all other sixth grade classes on the district's final assessment.

Yet, despite this highly successful student, most of my other students that year spent tons of time and effort on projects that taught them virtually nothing. No one could have taken an honest look at the 168 projects and concluded that they represented time well spent. However, most people never see the 168 disaster projects. They see the kids in ties and skirts standing in front of tri-fold boards. They see the newspaper articles and join the euphoria of the winners. Sexy and cheap.

Let's face it, the glow shines on us, too. The buzz and congratulations of Science Fair time catch us up in its spell. We start to believe that the congratulations might be warranted. We think, "that wasn't so bad…I'll do even better next year." So, the next year we start it all over again. Five minutes into it, we remember why Science Fair sucks.

In addition to district expectations and momentary lapses in sanity, we also do Science Fair because it feels like we should. Schools have been holding Science Fairs forever. Science Fair has deep roots in science teaching in America. My dad did Science Fair projects when he was a kid in the 1950s. How could schools get it so wrong for so long?

Moreover, other subjects assign projects, why not Science? Shouldn't we give our students long term assignments like the reports they get in English and the dioramas they do in social studies? Of course we should give these assignments as well. Right? (Actually, that's wrong. Science Fair isn't really an assignment…more on that later).

To sum up, we do Science Fair for three reasons. We do it because it's a cheap way to appear to address the need for reform. It allows adults at all levels of education to say we are investing in science education. We say this even though it costs the district nothing. It looks great to the public and costs nothing. Sexy and cheap. I think someone needs to look up the word "investment." Second, we do Science fair because on some level, as teachers, we believe the other grown-ups when they tell us we're doing a good job. Finally, we do Science Fair because it just seems like we should. It seems like a normal activity that has always happened in schools.

In the next chapter, we'll explore why Science Fair is actually a reverse investment, and why it's not like anything other teachers do in their classrooms. This has been a short chapter. I hope you do not feel ripped off. If you wish to know why it's so short, look back at the chapter title. Go ahead, do it now. How much could I really put into this chapter? Right?

5. Why We Should Stop Doing Science Fair. Now!

I always hoped that someday I would get twenty minutes with my principal to talk about Science Fair so I could tell this story… Imagine instead of running a school, you ran a large car company. Your company had several divisions, each making its own component for a variety of cars. One division made engines. Another made transmissions, etc…

Now imagine that one day one of your engineers said he had this great idea for a new component for the cars. This component would improve the cars in almost every way. With this new component, the cars would get better gas mileage. They would do zero to sixty quicker. The cars would cost less. Heck, the whole fleet would even have cup holders that actually worked.

You look at the specs of the cars with this new component and they totally wow you. So you ask how much it will cost. The engineer replies that it is all possible for a very modest investment of X dollars. You look at your profit margins and decide it can easily fit within the scope of the company's work. So you approve the component.

The excited engineer then spends the next year getting the new component off the ground. At the end of the year, you eagerly await the engineer's annual report. However, the engineer comes to you with disappointing news. They couldn't get the new component to work the way they wanted it to. They underestimated the difficulty of manufacturing it and bringing it to market. On the other hand, now that the new division has been through the process once, he has a much better idea of how to make it work.

You wonder for a moment. You hem and you haw. But then you remember those specs he showed you last year. Man, an automobile fleet like that would KILL the competition. So you ask what it will take to make it happen for next year. The engineer replies that it will cost Y additional dollars on top of last year's investment. You look at your company's bottom line and see that it would eat up pretty much all of your profits, but wouldn't tap into the productivity of the other divisions. It's a lot but...those specs! You green light round two.

At the end of the year, the engineer comes back with more disappointing news. The additional infusion of cash did realize improvements to the component. However, they were modest to say the least. The component still hasn't made it into production models. Ugh, you think...and there goes your profit margins for the year. The investors are going to be ticked!

The engineer says that a little more investment will do the trick. Now you really wonder because you've eaten up last year's profits on this component. What else can you do? He suggests that you take a small amount out of the budget from the other divisions and use it to make the final modifications to the new component. This seems risky. You make good cars as it is. Do you really want to put a strain on the other divisions? Will this compromise your existing line-up?

The engineer shows you the spec sheet again and you start to drool. Okay. One more year. When this new component goes into production, the payoff will be so profound none of these "growing pains" will matter. You agree and send the bad news to the other divisions. Cutbacks. You promise them it'll be temporary and that the payoff will be huge.

One year later, you wait for the report from the engineer. You're sweating this time because the cars that came off the line this year had issues. The cutbacks really hurt. Reliability went down. The media got hold of a few high profile safety failures. Sales declined. The company is in real trouble. Now you're making substandard cars and the company has gone into the red.

It won't matter, though. When that engineer comes through that office door, sits in that chair across your desk, and hands you a cigar, you'll light it, take a puff, and then cough for ten minutes straight. Then laugh your butt off.

The engineer strides in, sits across from you, and waits. You say, "Well? Give me some good news."

He replies, "I have good news. The new investment has made some modest improvements possible and with just a little more, I think we can finally get this done right."

You fly off the roof. "A little more," you shout. "We're already spending almost as much as we do on a whole car! How much can we spend on this new component of yours?"

"But the specs," he reminds you.

"To heck with the specs," you respond. "Let's just see what this miracle component is all about. Take me to the plant."

So you fly out to Detroit to see exactly what this little component that has cost your company so much is really about. When you get to the factory that's been manufacturing it you realize exactly what's been happening. They have not been manufacturing a simple component to add to their existing cars in order to improve them. They've been manufacturing a whole new car.

Your blood boils. "What's this? I thought you were making a component, not a whole new car?"

"Well," responds the engineer, "it started out that way, but each year we needed to add more and more on to it to make it work until we'd practically added a whole car."

Now you understand, no component could ever achieve the stats that you and the engineer had drooled over. It seemed like it could be done. In the end, though, a whole new car had to be built. In doing so, you've compromised all the other divisions, started producing junky cars, and flushed your company down the toilet.

If this engineer had come to you originally with a plan to build a whole new car, there's no way you would have approved it. The expense would have been too great. You knew the other divisions couldn't support the addition of another complete vehicle. However, now it's too late. You report the bad news at the next shareholders meeting and are quickly tarred and feathered.

I'd love to tell this story to my principal someday. Maybe the analogy would explain it better than science teachers have been trying to explain it to principals for generations. Here's how I'd end the story.

"The car company is your science program and the component is Science Fair."

Any sane manager would kill this component. At best a small study group would form to investigate ways to manufacture the component without trashing the company. Whatever happens, though, the other divisions, the successful ones, have to be saved. Kill the component. Stop the bleeding. Now!

At a bare minimum cancel Science Fair. Empower a small group to study and revise it or something. If they're honest, they'll come up with a lot of the stuff you've read about in this book. However, if you want to stop reading now, go ahead and stop. Cancel your fair. It's the least you can do for your students. Save your science program. Stop the bleeding. Or...read on and find out how we saved our Science Fair and didn't kill our whole program.

6. The Stop the Bleeding Approach

One year, at a previous school, I convinced my principal to make some significant changes to the way we did Science Fair. I wish I could say that I used rational arguments about why Science Fair fails by design year after year. I didn't though. I had to get at it through a back door.

Students in our district have had stubbornly low standardized test scores in middle school Science. Moreover, they have failed to make the gains that they have shown in math and English. The head of the Science department in my district had crunched some numbers and had told me that students who received a seventy percent or better on the district end-of-year assessment in eighth grade went on to pass the state's high stakes test at the end of middle school.

Armed with this analysis I made an argument to my principal. If we focus unwaveringly on our curriculum (which the district end-of-year assessment was based on), then we could finally crack the high stakes testing nut. When she asked me what this meant, I suggested that we had to cut out or greatly reduce the non-curriculum activities in which we engaged. I named a few harmless things that no one would miss too much. She nodded. Then I dropped the S-bomb: Science Fair.

After a long pause she countered that parents would resist this change as they'd come to expect it at the school. This represented the inertia of Science Fair rearing its ugly head. It's hard to imagine a world without Science Fair.

Frankly, it was hard for me too. Even though Science Fair completely failed for ninety-five percent of the students, there were a few who got a lot out of it. These were the kids who loved Science already and had a lot of support at home. They really could get Science Fair to work for them. How could we deprive them of the experience?

My seventh and eighth grade colleague and I had thought this through, though. We had a plan. I offered to my principal in that meeting that we really didn't want to eliminate the benefits these few students experienced. So, we would transform Science Fair into an after-school club. We would build it up as a prestige with the students. We'd tell them that if they wanted to join, they'd have to fill out an application and space would be limited to thirty (out of three hundred middle schoolers). Really, though, we would take anyone who wanted to join. My principal reluctantly agreed.

Before I get into how we structured the club, let me skip to the end and tell you the profound impact this had on our middle school. That year I finished teaching the district curriculum in its entirety for the first time in my career. Nothing was cut. Moreover, astoundingly, my students outperformed all other sixth grade classes in the city on the district end-of-year assessment...by a lot!

That alone represents dramatic big news, but this next result totally knocked my socks off. It's actually knocking my socks of right now just thinking about it. Ready? Compared to the previous year on the state high stakes exam, our group of failing eighth graders shrank by twelve percent. Let me repeat that: twelve percent fewer kids failed. That's huge. Districts make gigantic investments in math and English and don't see results like that. We did it in science for free.

Now here's the double whammy. The year after that the group of failing students dropped by another twenty-five percent. These represented the first two years, we saw gains in eighth grade Science test scores. The positive returns of ending Science Fair compounded year over year. Moreover, we didn't have to invest a dime. We didn't do anything new. We just stopped doing something stupid: Science Fair.

Go back and re-read the last three paragraphs. You can stop reading this book now, if you'd like. However, let me just say that I didn't stay at that school forever, and I found another solution in a new school. So, at minimum, put this book down and go cancel your Science Fair. Read a little more if you're interested in how we structured our Science Fair club. Finish if you want to see how we cracked Science Fair in a totally different (and better) way in my new school.

The club was pretty simple. We created an application for students to fill out. We told them it would be limited to thirty students. We had about twenty applicants and we accepted them all. We had one organizational after-school meeting with the whole club at the beginning, then another half way through and a final one before the Science Fair event.

Here's the magic part. I actually had many more mini-meetings. Students could sign up for an after-school meeting with me any time they wanted. This allowed me to give the individually tailored, one-on-one support to each student that I could never do for 168 kids. Moreover, they got the support exactly when they needed it instead of when I could squeeze in a class lesson. Their learning benefited as a result.

By the end of the club, every single project was Science Fair worthy. Moreover, because we had a small subset of our overall population, we could send all of them to the city-wide fair. The academic and emotional payoff for them was huge.

This represented a true win-win. The general population of students learned more and better science as evidenced by district and state test scores. The small subset who benefited from Science Fair, got to do Science Fair. I got to focus my energies on improving Science achievement for my students AND give one-on-one support to students who really got juiced by Science Fair. In addition, my school data looked great. It's amazing how much healing you can do if you just stop the bleeding.

You're probably wondering if, after the numbers came in, district level people came pounding at my classroom door to ask me to train other teachers in my "innovative" teaching techniques that proved so successful with my students. If such an occasion had happened, I would have saved them tons of money just by telling them to cancel Science Fair and let teachers teach the curriculum. Nope.

In fact, in subsequent years, pressure increased to provide every child with a Science Fair experience. This became such a district mantra that after my principal left, a new one came and insisted we re-start Science Fair as a whole school endeavor. I left that school shortly thereafter. Guess what happened to their test scores?

7. Why We (actually) Shouldn't Stop Doing Science Fair

I've spent a lot of time and words explaining why Science Fair fails and the huge gains you can realize by just cutting it from the curriculum and starting a club. This change will liberate huge amounts of time and resources to devote to teaching science content. That stuff matters a lot. The more content students can master, the more robust their conceptual framework in science. Then, as they grow through their formal education and into the rest of their lives, they can grapple with all the new science and tech that will come their way. They will have the conceptual tools to contend with new and important science information.

However, when it comes right down to it, process matters too. It's easy to dismiss this, in light of the amount of content we need to teach. Kids need to know so many concepts! However, science isn't just something students need to know, it's something they need to do. Kids need to know how to do science. All the concepts they need to learn were first discovered because someone did some science and discovered them. Like my supervisor's T-shirt says…"Science is a Verb."

We often feel we can teach good process through the content we're already engaging in. If we use a good inquiry curriculum, the process is built right in. Right? Well…sort of. A great science teacher colleague of mine, Bob Ettinger, once told me "the research out there says you can teach kids hard content and you can teach them hard process. But you can't teach both at once." Since we focus so much on teaching hard content, we often teach an "express" version of the process.

We may ask kids to design an investigation to prove whether or not air has mass. However, how much process can you teach if they have forty-seven minutes to come up with the experiment, carry it out, and draw a conclusion based on their observations? We're satisfied if they sketch out an idea to fill one balloon with air, leave another empty, and put them on the ends of a homemade seesaw. Yes, they learn the confounding concept that air actually does have mass. However, at best, we would call this "Scientific Method - Light."

Don't get me wrong. Kids do need to look at evidence and draw a conclusion. We're good at teaching this way. However, we typically do it in highly structured situations. We guide the process very precisely to insure that students will see the data or results that will allow them to make the content connections. I'm not knocking content connections. We help them make good, deep content connections that often require rigorous, high order thinking. However, the thinking is all about content. We limit their struggles with process so they can make the leaps in content.

If we're always teaching "hard science content," however, we'll never get to the "hard science process." Content matters a lot, but students need a time when they can grapple and struggle with process, also. They do need to know a lot of science, but they need to know how to DO science, too. Science is a verb. Process matters. Figuring out how to go about gaining evidence to prove a hypothesis is hard. It requires failure and reiteration. It takes reflection and self-analysis. It takes time, feedback, revision, repetition. In short...it takes teaching. Bing! Light bulb.

8. How To Do Science Fair So It Works For Your Students AND You (and maybe even your school and district)

Teaching Science Fair takes teaching. Everything kids need to learn takes teaching. Why would we think about Science Fair in any other way? We give them the assignment and expect them to step up. We never teach them how to do it, though. We never teach them how to do the process of science.

This idea seems simple but it took me years before it finally hit me over the head and made me see it. Science Fair is not an assignment. It's a curriculum. Curriculum needs to be taught. No amount of improved direction, rubrics, exemplars, timelines, checklists, or increasingly thick packets can replace teaching. I hate this word but, duh.

I started thinking about Science Fair as a unit to teach in class that would start with simple concepts and build, with scaffolding up to a complete experiment. To do this I had to let some things go and think of others in a new way. This was hard because it seemed less like Science Fair. That's okay, though. My experience with traditional Science Fair was one of abject failure. If what I tried to do seemed less like that, then…all the better.

First, I let go of the idea that every student had to choose his or her own question to investigate. "But that's the whole point of Science Fair!" If you just thought that, go back and read the previous 8,000 or so words. The old way sucks for kids, teachers, schools, districts, America, and the world. Maybe more.

Teach the same thing to everyone. We teach everything else this way. In math class, we don't teach one student single digit multiplication, and another reducing fractions and still another the long division algorithm all at the same time. We would teach each of these concepts to all students at once, one at a time. This allows teachers to maximize effort and impact.

I started to think about Science Fair the same way. If each student chose their own question, then each student would require a different series of lessons to create meaningful hypotheses, detailed procedures, etc... Each student would get stuck at different places thinking about different things and need different supports. This type of teaching requires a tutoring model and is not possible when multiplied by one hundred fifty students. So, I let it go. We would all investigate a variation of the same question. Thus, experimental designs would be similar and support could be given to the whole class while small groups could be coached in a workshop scenario. I could adopt a differentiated instruction model rather than an individual tutor model. Okay, this is starting to sound like teaching now.

Then, I had to let go of another sacred cow: content. I had to jettison the idea that students would learn any type of profound or meaningful content by doing their experiment. It's the process, stupid. I would use simple content and allow the hard work to go into the process. That's where we'd spend our time. The content is irrelevant. (I have to admit, it still hurts a little to write those words).

Next, I taught in reverse. Often I have observed content being taught like this: teachers provide procedures and a set of materials that students work through to get the results necessary to make content leaps. Reverse that. Agree on the goal and show them the materials they have available to meet that goal. Then students can cooperatively struggle through the process. Therefore, ultimately, if they don't reach the goal of their experiment, they still may nail the whole point of the unit. After all, the lesson was about the process, not if they, indeed, proved their hypothesis. If a student says an experiment was inconclusive AND can explain why and how they could change their design to get better data...they win. So do you.

***

Another "aha moment" came when I realized that a Science Fair experiment is an interdisciplinary endeavor by its nature. In order to accomplish the experiment successfully, students must draw on knowledge from all the academic disciplines. They must determine a testable question, form a hypothesis, and design an inquiry. These skills come from the domain of Science. However, they also use math skills to analyze the data, language skills to write portions of their report, and research skills in doing their background research. (We even found a connection with Latin class. More on that later). Why not work with other content teachers where appropriate to "interdisciplinize" the project. Students would use skills and knowledge from all their classes in the service of determining some truth. It may be a small truth. It may represent content that is elementary or even irrelevant to the greater scientific community. But, hey, it's their own and they're only twelve-years old.

No matter what type of experiment your students end up doing, they will have to gather data along the way. This data is recorded in a notebook. I call these notebooks "Science Fair Journals" to avoid confusion with the myriad other "notebooks" students carry around. However, in addition to gathering their data, they must also analyze the data. This may involve concepts such as graphing, statistical significance, creating meaningful tables, applying various statistical analysis, interpolation, extrapolation, outliers, etc... Math teachers work very hard with students on these concepts. Why not use data that the students generated themselves to provide context! This can infuse meaning and motivation into the instruction.

Math teachers have busy days just like us, though. We don't want to shove extra work on them. When I worked with teachers on my team, I emphasized that we should put Science Fair to work for our students and us. So, since the math teacher on my team had been working on bar graphs vs. line plots, she ended up attacking the data from that angle. Any angle of attack works as long as it maximizes teacher impact on student learning.

I worked with the social studies teacher (called Humanities in my school) on the background research portion of the experiment. Once again, social studies teachers teach a myriad of concepts regarding library (and now Internet) research. My teammate wanted to work on distinguishing legitimate vs. Illegitimate sources on the Internet. She used Science Fair to teach this. She spent time teaching and assessing the students and when they were done, they used their research to advance their science experiment. She did a much better job at this than I could have because she's put much more time into teaching this content.

Moreover, students do writing in multiple forms for their project. They do argumentative writing for the conclusion. They learn and practice this type of writing in English class. They also write an abstract for their paper, which summarizes their whole experiment. While abstract writing does not fall within the English curriculum, it's not far off. The abstract can be tailored to fit into work students do anyway in English class.

Big Picture: Science experimentation is an interdisciplinary endeavor by nature. If we treat it as such we can really use it to tie together learning across disciplines. If we do it right, we can put Science Fair to work for us instead of enslaving us (and by extension our students) to Science Fair. It can be a curriculum around which our whole team coalesces and thrives. It can also advance the content of each academic domain.

***

This next "aha" represents a short but important part of this book. Don't parallel teach. Remember, Science Fair is a curriculum not an assignment. You wouldn't teach the structures of the cell and Newton's Laws at the same time. That would be silly.

Instead, you'd create a series of lessons on the cell. Perhaps you'd have students use microscopes. Maybe they'd sketch what they saw. Maybe you'd have them hunt for and identify differences between leaf cells and their own cheek cells. They could make diagrams, posters, charts, Venn diagrams etc. Then, when they'd been summatively assessed on that content, students would start rolling miniature cars down ramps and timing them with stop watches to discover the laws of motion. Different content. Different time. Different units. That's how we teach everything else.

This year I taught Science Fair the same way. When I taught Science Fair, I taught nothing else. I didn't squeeze in a mini-assignment here and there in the last ten minutes of class. Science Fair got its own parcel of complete time. I didn't try to teach it at the same time I taught students how to analyze the sand in various sand stones.

It's amazing how this is all just really basic teaching. It just required me to see that one of the giant reasons Science Fair sucked was that it was a whole curriculum that I had been treating as an assignment. Teaching content and teaching Science Fair required different pedagogy. Once I realized this, I could break it down like any other unit.

To summarize:
1. Things to Let Go of:
    - Every student chooses a unique question to investigate
    - They will learn rigorous content by doing their experiment (It's the process, stupid!)
2. Teach in Reverse
3. Teach interdisciplinary
4. Involve other content teachers
5. Don't parallel teach

9. But Wait. What About the Whole Purpose of Science Fair?

When I talk to people about changing Science Fair so that it's not a complete disaster and abject failure, they respond with what became the title of this short chapter. Let's take a moment on this topic. First, if you read the first sentence of this chapter and saw the words "complete disaster" and "abject failure" and thought..."amen, brother," then we wouldn't need this chapter at all. Why would we keep doing something that we associate with those words?

I'll take apart what folks often mean when they talk about "the whole purpose of Science Fair." "Science Fair is supposed to represent independent work on the student's part. You've got them working in groups!" If the point of traditional Science Fair is independent work then...fail. They can't work on this independently because they don't know how to. The reason they don't know how to work independently is they've never been taught to. Science Fair is not an assignment, it's a curriculum, and should be taught that way. In my neck of the woods, that means...workshop model. I teach all my other science in small groups working collaboratively with coaching from me. This represents pedagogy with tons of research behind it. Why would we teach Science Fair differently? Science process is hard! We should teach it with the best methods we know.

"But Science Fair is a chance for students to apply what they know to their own project." As mentioned above, they don't know this yet. They have nothing to apply. They have a packet of directions, checklists, and rubrics. They don't have the skills attained from rigorous academic instruction over time. They need to learn Science Fair (i.e. The Scientific Method) before they can apply it.

When I say "learn," I don't mean that they can recite the steps using a clever mnemonic device. I mean they've been explicitly taught using best pedagogical practices. They've had the opportunity to construct meaning around scientific process based on classroom experiences. They've had a time when the content didn't matter because the process was the content.

"But Science Fair is finally a student's chance to pursue something that actually interests them because they get to choose it." Hogwash. They don't take interest in it. In fact, they hate it because they don't know how to do it and it's turning most kids off to science...maybe for life. More often than not, they find some boilerplate "experiment" on the Internet and go through the motions. Science Fair, as traditionally conceived, has the exact opposite effect on students as the one desired by utterers of the topic sentence of this paragraph. Science Fair kills enthusiasm for science.

In sum, the "whole purpose of Science Fair" never really existed. None of these reasons for doing Science Fair ever enter into the picture for almost all students when we go about it in the traditional manner. Because students have had little formal instruction in the process of science, they don't get a meaningful independent experience with Science Fair. Moreover, a Science Fair project fails to provide an opportunity for application because, once again, they've had little formal instruction and therefore little to apply. Lastly, Science Fair does not give students a chance to, "finally" work on something that interests them personally. They don't know how to apply the method meaningfully and stumble through it, hating it the whole time. If you don't believe me, ask them. Also, if you're a high school teacher ask students if they'd be more likely to take a science elective if they knew they wouldn't have to do a Science Fair project. I've tried it. Guess what most kids say?

10. How We Remade Science Fair for 7th Graders (The Background Work)

In my school, we came up with our plan to change Science Fair at the beginning of my fourth year here. The previous three years I'd had many conversations with many science teachers in the school. I had even more with science teachers around the district over the previous eight years. These conversations ranged from ranting about Science Fair to working with a small team to come up with a complete seven-year plan to reform Science Fair for grades 7-12 in my current school. We based our plan on some of the data you've read about in this book. We presented it to our department head who met it with enthusiasm. However, for a variety of reasons, it went exactly nowhere. The next year, the status quo remained.

Our department head was new and, having been an eighth grade science teacher the year before, had experienced the disaster of Science Fair herself. Moreover, she was open to change. However, our seventh through twelfth grade reform plan called for one elective course to be created in the upper grades. In addition, the effort would require quite a bit of coordination throughout the school. The elective could not be squeezed into our budget and reorganizing Science Fair for a whole school was not exactly an overnight task.

So, it became clear that if I wanted to fix Science Fair, I would have to start it myself in my classroom. I had a brainstorm session with my department head. We created the briefest outline of the basic plan. Do the project in class. Every student does a variation of the same experiment. Teach it like we'd teach any other curriculum using the best teaching strategies we know. Finally, make it an interdisciplinary project. So the experiment would "live" in all the students' classrooms.

Next, the other seventh grade science teacher and I scheduled a meeting with the department head to elaborate a more specific plan. I called the three of us the "Science Squad." In this meeting, we decided what our Science Fair would look like. We chose "plants" as a topic. We picked plants because we knew that students could observe changes and collect data over time. Moreover, the data would be quantitative and they could use a variety of analytic tools to crunch the numbers later.

Now we had an idea of the broad outlines of the experiment that students would do. They would plant seeds. Each group of plants would have a different variable applied to it. Students would measure the growth of their experimental plants and compare them to the growth of some control plants.

This meeting also resulted in a timeline for the project. We roughly planned when we would complete each part of the experiment and when it would "visit" each content teacher. From choosing an independent variable to presenting their findings, students would work on this project from October through late December. They would complete experimentation and presentation by Winter vacation. This left plenty of time before our school-wide Science Fair where the best projects competed for a spot at the city-wide fair.

After this initial meeting, my seventh grade partner and I scheduled twenty-minute after-school meetings every couple of weeks. We did this because that's all the time we had. She had to pick up a child from school and had a hard deadline to leave each day. This proved to be enough. At each of the meetings, we answered the questions that came up during implementation and planned accordingly. I found these meetings hugely helpful because my partner had good questions that I hadn't thought of. Moreover, I work much faster when I can bounce ideas off another person or build on their ideas.

We both had several questions to address right off the bat such as… What kind of plants should we use to provide the greatest chance of success? How much space would this take up? How would we keep the plants alive long enough to gather data? What about timing to introduce, prepare a plan, plant seeds, and tend to the plants on a regular basis? How will we organize students to do the work? What type of "fair" will we have when the day comes? What about all that grading? How will we collaborate with the other content teachers? This list of questions became our starting point. We answered each one before we began. Here's what we came up with…

First, we puzzled through a few options for what type of plant to use. My first instinct pointed to beans. I could buy one bag of lima beans at the grocery store for less than two dollars and have enough seeds for all of my one-hundred forty students. Moreover, a bean seed has such a large cotyledon that they grew easily even with imperfect care. However, beans grow either very tall (pole beans) or very bushy (bush beans). This could prove difficult given the lack of space in my classroom. In addition, the fact that the initial growth of beans largely relies on its own store of food from within the seed, meant that the variables students applied may have little affect. Perhaps beans wouldn't fit the bill. If you've got the space and time, though, they might make a great plant to study.

We sought a smaller plant that we could more easily subject to a variety of variables. I thought about grass. Grass seeds had a very small cotyledon and therefore less food to get it going. It would be more dependent on how students cared for it and therefore might display more change when subjected to variables. As a gardener, I gravitated toward winter rye grass. In my garden, I broadcast the seeds in the fall and walk away. They grow tall by the time Spring comes. If winter doesn't kill the plants, they might just hold up to middle schoolers!

Moreover, this plant satisfied my space requirements. Winter rye does not climb poles or sprout large leaves. It grows strait up and we can plant many seeds in a small place. So, instead of having flower pots on every available surface in my room, I could use small six-pack sprouters. These are the things you get in May when you're buying cucumber and basil sprouts to put in your garden. They take up very little space and have room for six "trials" for the students. I have five sections of students with seven groups of four per section. So that means I need room for thirty-five six-pack sprouters. Not too bad. I also found trays that could hold several of the six-packs. All told I fit all my student's experimental six-packs in three sprouter trays. My room consists of fourteen long tables with two students per table. I placed the sprouters on the side of three of the tables closest to the window. So, using grass and the small sprouters solved the space problem. Moreover, each experiment could have six "trials."

Having solved the plant species and space issue, we moved onto time. How would we organize our time to teach the necessary skills and concepts? We decided to devote a block of days up front to Science Fair. In these days students would explore the idea behind the experiment, choose a variable, debate, and decide on a procedure, a data collection method, etc… For more details on how I structured this time, see the lesson materials included in the appendices.

We had to address more time issues, though. In addition to planning time for puzzling through and setting up the experiment, we had to figure out a way for the students to keep the plants alive and make measurements as the plants grew. We decided to devote five or so minutes every few days to plant care and measurement. This fit in to how we already structured our class time. Each day we began class with a "Do Now" assignment. It's a short 5-10 minute activity (usually a warm-up question) to start the class off working on the day's topic. We decided that every few days the students would water and measure their grass for their "Do Now." After the first few times, this became a quick and easy portion of class. This allowed us to continue our experiment and move on to another unit of study.

Next, my grade partner and I tackled how we'd structure student grouping. Ultimately, we chose to use the same structure we used for all our teaching. Students worked in teams of four. So each team would select a variable to apply to the rye grass and set up one six-pack seed sprouter. They'd collaborate to determine a procedure and define their measurement protocol. They would work together to collect the data. So students accomplished much of the work collaboratively, just like they did for most of their science work in school.

However, we built in individual work as well. Each student kept his or her own Science Fair journal. In this journal, they would record all the ideas their team agreed on for setting up their experiment (question, procedure, etc.). They'd each also do their own background research and record it in this Journal. As each part of the project came due, each student would submit a final version individually. For example, while a group would puzzle through how to set up their experiment (the procedure) each student submitted their own complete, written out procedure. The basic idea for all four students ended up being the same, but the amount of detail, thought and specificity was up to individual student effort. In addition, when students completed the experiment, each student wrote their own conclusion, which I individually assessed.

As you can see, we really had to let go of a lot of our Science Fair baggage to work this way. However, we still needed to accomplish some type of "Fair" and select students to compete at the whole school and possibly city-wide level. Rather than have students set up the classic tri-fold boards and display them as others walked around and judged, we decided that students would create a Google presentation. Students would present their experiments in teams. I used a rubric that allowed me to assess each individual student's contribution to the presentation. We called it a virtual Science Fair.

The virtual fair has several advantages. First, it was an opportunity for me to teach the students some "twenty-first century skills." We worked in class on creating Google slide shows, and on working as a team "in the cloud." They could more easily accomplish work outside of school because they didn't need to rely on their parents or public transportation to meet face-to-face. They could all work on the Google slides document simultaneously and communicate via "chat" as they worked. After our "Fair" when each group presented their investigation, I used my assessment of their final paper and their portion of the presentation to choose two students per class to compete in the school-wide fair. These students then transformed their virtual presentation into a traditional tri-fold board.

We also spent some time figuring out how we would tackle all that grading. It could easily take ten minutes to grade a traditional Science Fair project. Reading each final paper, flipping through each Science

Fair journal, and checking each tri-fold board represented a very labor-intensive process. Add to that the frustration of realizing how much work you and the students had done and how little there was to show for it and you had a recipe for tears. Now, however, the projects showed real learning. I still spent a lot of time grading, but the effort seemed much more fruitful.

Moreover, we built in some strategies to spread out the grading. First, we graded each portion of the experiment as students completed it. For example, students would submit their procedures long before they finished the experiment. I would grade them early. I built a spreadsheet to record the grades of each portion of the project (procedure, background research, data, etc.). When we finished Science Fair, the spreadsheet would tally the scores for each portion to come up with a final score for the whole paper. I would grade the presentation on-the-fly using a rubric and a spreadsheet as students gave them. I would also have the students "share" their Google presentations with me so I could go back and check out portions if I needed to. So, while we would still spend a lot of time grading, we'd able to do it in smaller chunks and, hopefully, since the work would show real learning, it wouldn't seem like the wasted effort we always confronted with traditional Science Fair.

Moreover, as mentioned earlier, the Science Squad envisioned this as an interdisciplinary event. Some portions of the project would live in other classrooms. I would work with each teacher individually as the project moved on. For example, when students completed data collection in my class, I'd work with the math teacher on how to advance the students along. We would need to discuss issues such as what the data would look like when students came with it to her class, what should we expect from students when they completed the analysis, etc. The math teacher would then work with students on analyzing their data. This would result in some type of data display and discussion. The math teacher could enter the grade she gave students on this work directly into the spreadsheet I made. So the students' "data" grade would tally automatically into their final paper. I'll get more into the interdisciplinary angle later.

11. Making It Happen

Once we'd answered our background questions and had a handle on the scope of the project, we needed to implement it. Since the Science Squad had envisioned this as an interdisciplinary event, we first needed to pitch it to our grade level teams. We wanted to get ideas and feedback from the other content teachers. After all, in this new version of Science Fair, it would be their project, too!

The basis of the pitch represented an essential (but typically unacknowledged) truth about science. Scientific investigation is an inherently interdisciplinary endeavor. Students will use skills and knowledge from across their domains of learning to accomplish it. This is true for middle school students and university professors alike. This project is bigger than one classroom.

It was important to me that this project was not just a burden to put on already overworked colleagues' shoulders. Moreover, it also didn't make sense for this to represent an interruption of students' learning in other classes. "Hey kids I know we're studying polynomials, but let's work on graphing for the next few days." I wanted to put Science Fair to work for students and teachers, not enslave them to it. So, I explained Science Fair as a way for students to contextualize the learning they were already doing in each of their classes by grounding that learning in actual experiences they had throughout the investigation in science class. Math students would have their own numbers to crunch that had real world meaning to them. Social studies students could do research that they could put into actual use in a real physical problem they grappled with. Language Arts students could produce persuasive writing about something they figured out themselves using evidence they generated via their own investigation.

Big picture: students use all of their academic skills in service of discovery. Moreover, it's their discovery. It's their little piece of truth: a truth behind which to put all of their academic learning. One of the essential questions that my seventh grade team uses to teach students revolves around "determining truth." This project allowed students to connect to that essential question in all their classes in a unified way. Moreover, through the leadership of our Language Arts teachers, we connected this project to a yearlong theme that students engaged with: "Making the World a Better Place." That theme, however, is a much bigger matter, and a topic for another book.

Once we'd hammered out a general outline of how the project would flow, I took the reins and introduced the project to my five classes of seventh grade general science students. I shall describe how the process unfolded in the classroom; however, for more details you can check out the lesson outlines and supporting materials in the appendices.

On the first day, I contextualized the project. The students would study grass. Why? Because, as described earlier, we could fit it in the classroom, it grew in harsh conditions, and could withstand "care" given by a twelve-year-old. As you can imagine, seventh graders might not find that very exciting. Grass, however, does represent a huge and crucial link in the human food chain. Eighty-four million acres of land in the United States is devoted to the growing of corn. Another 46 million acres are used for growing wheat. Add to that the growing of rice, barley and other grains. All of these crops are grasses. When confronted with these facts, many of my students argued that they eat a lot of meat, not grains. The answer to this, of course, is that a huge portion of cattle and livestock feed is corn based. A huge portion of the food chain has corn, rice, and wheat in it somewhere. So, the growing of grass represents no trivial matter in sustaining human life on earth.

Next, I tied these facts to our seventh grade year-long theme: "Making the world a better place." I gave students a homework assignment to brainstorm a list of things they normally throw away that they believe might improve the growing of grass. This assignment would represent the "seed" of their experiment (please forgive the pun. I couldn't help myself).

The next day we collected all their ideas. When they returned to class students volunteered the items from their brainstorm and we made a list of what would become potential independent variables. They had items like, used coffee grounds, tea bags, rice, spaghetti, beans, paper, etc. Mostly they came up with food that they often throw away in their homes. Thus, the assignment provided students with an opportunity to bring culturally relevant items into the classroom. They could base their experiment on trash from their own lives.

This resulted in a huge list of items that students could use as an independent variable to apply to the grass they would grow. However, before I had students choose one item, I provided the scientific structure they'd use to proceed with their experiment. I taught them the format we'd use to frame their investigation: the testable question. All the students would use a variation of the same question: How does _____ affect the growth of rye grass? I explained that each team of four students would debate and choose one of the items to explore. We discussed that this would be their independent variable and defined what that meant.

Students chose variables in groups. This did not always go perfectly smoothly. Some teams agreed fairly easily. Some had a difficult time coming to agreement. I used it as an opportunity to teach collaborative work: an important twenty-first century learning goal.

Once teams had chosen a variable, and used it to create a testable question, I introduced the Science Fair journal. Students recorded every aspect of their experiment in the journal. In the past, I had required students to procure their own notebook to use for this purpose. However, this year I bought one hundred fifty blue exam books and distributed one to each student. This solved a few problems. First, each year a significant group of students couldn't get their hands on a notebook. These students always got a late start as I played phone tag with their parents to track down the reason and hold them accountable. I always ended up buying notebooks anyway for some students. Second, the projects would not take up a whole notebook. It seemed like a waste to make students buy a whole notebook for one project. The blue exam books have about 16 pages to write on. This proved to be plenty of space to collect all our Science Fair related information.

It didn't end up costing me anything. I charged each student one dollar for the blue exam books. This amount covered the Science Fair journals plus all the other materials (seeds, soil, sprouters, pipettes, etc). So, in the end, it cost me nothing and each student did a whole project for only one dollar in materials. That's much less money than a student would spend on a traditional Science Fair project. Heck, that's less than they'd normally spend on the notebook alone.

Once everyone had a notebook, I directed the students in formatting it. First, they set up the cover with their names and relevant personal information. I explained how a scientist used a lab notebook and that they would use use their Science Fair journals in the same way. They'd record everything they did for the project in the journal and date every entry whenever they used it. They'd start by writing down their independent variable and why they chose it. Moreover, they would record their testable question. This represented all the work the students had done so far. So they each now had an up-to-date journal.

Now that they knew their topic and had picked an independent variable and question, the project left my room and went to the social studies teacher. In order for students to come up with a more informed hypothesis, they would need to research their topic. I met with the social studies teacher to work out how to structure this research. Once again, I thought it was important for this to work for the students in terms of their learning goals for social studies. I wanted the teacher to put Science Fair to work for her and her students not enslave them to it.

One of the social studies learning goals for students was to be able to find, use, source, and evaluate the validity of resources they used for research. So, she used Science Fair to teach this content. In the end, she had students brainstorm ten questions whose answers would make them more knowledgeable on their Science Fair topic. This new knowledge would help them form a hypothesis to address their testable question. Then, they picked two of those questions and spent two days in the school library and on the internet researching answers. They took notes on what they found in their Science Fair journals, and summarized their findings in a short write-up, which they turned into their social studies teacher for a grade. She evaluated their write-ups based on her goals for their learning.

Their research gave them quite an array of background knowledge. Some wrote about the details of photosynthesis. Many explored various soil nutrients and their relationship to the functioning of plants. Others uncovered information about decomposition and the use of compost in gardening. Some found useful information about potentially helpful nutrients in their independent variables (e.g. Calcium in eggshells). Between all the students, they had a hefty knowledge about plants.

Some of this information became extremely relevant in their investigations. For many the research led them down a blind alley. However, for almost all students, I saw a boost in confidence and engagement with the project. They were applying information they'd worked hard to come by to a real experiment they were doing. At the end of the whole Science Fair process, it would turn out that despite their increase in background knowledge, many of their hypotheses would prove wrong, or the experiment would go awry. That was okay, though, because that just creates more questions to answer. If they recognized these questions and could imagine a new way of approaching the experiment and expressed motivation to engage in a second iteration, then you win. Big time. Moreover, in science, questions are good because they lead to more science. If we had all the answers it would put scientists out of work!

After they'd done their research, the project returned to the science classroom so students could form their hypotheses. I introduced them to the the way I wanted them to write their hypotheses. Students would create hypotheses in this form: If_____then_____because_____.

I'd been using an exemplar Science Fair project to model the process up to this point. I had found a project about determining the affect of water on the growth of bread mold. This project had the following hypothesis: If I place two pieces of bread in two bags, and I add water to one, then the bread with water will grow mold faster because all living things require water to live and mold is a living thing. As you can see, the hypothesis provides a basic structure for an experiment. This format for the hypothesis also includes the research that led to the hypothesis after the "because."

Students then made hypotheses of their own. I had them first work in their teams to debate predictions about how their independent variable would affect the growth of their winter rye grass. They had each done independent research, so they could each bring reasons to back up their predictions. It was very rewarding to watch them defend their predictions with such vigor. They each had special knowledge about plant growth that gave every student a slightly different expertise. So in a way, they were defending a part of themselves. I saw fantastic buy-in. This alone represented a huge leap from previous versions of Science Fair where students hate every step of the process. Now they jumped at the opportunity to prove themselves correct.

At the end of the day, I did not require each team to come to consensus on a hypothesis. How could I? That would invalidate the expertise they'd acquired through research and destroy the engagement they had created. I found it important, though for students to hear and evaluate the ideas of other students. At the conclusion of this lesson, students had each written a hypothesis in a new Science Fair journal entry and could back up their prediction with researched evidence.

Next, the students would begin to imagine and plan their experiment. So, I introduced the purpose of their science experiments (of all science experiments): to gather data that would support or refute their hypotheses. They needed to figure out what to do to get that data. So students worked in teams to outline an idea about what they'd do. I would visit the teams and support them by asking questions to guide their thinking. The teams came up with variations on the same general idea. Plant some grass seeds. Add the item they'd chosen as an independent variable. Then measure the plants as they grow.

This was very reminiscent of the "Scientific Method - Light" they usually applied when the content was the point. However, now we focused on process. So I showed them the materials they'd have available: a six-pack seed sprouter, rye grass seeds, potting soil, rulers, graduated cylinders, pipettes and hand lenses. I asked them to work in teams to brainstorm a procedure to follow in order to set up their experiment. Time to get specific. As they worked I checked in with them and continued to probe with questions, pushing them to think deeper about how to organize their experiment to get useful data.

I recognized a lack of a control group in most teams' ideas. So, I brought us together as a whole class and we shared out. Several groups volunteered their ideas so far. They still had the basic structure of plant seeds, add variable, and measure, but contained more specifics about when and how to use the materials I had shown them. I then chose one group's example and asked students to imagine the experiment was complete and that the plants the students had grown were now fifteen centimeters tall. I asked who could tell me, based on this data, if their variable helped the plant grow or not. A student volunteered that it did help the plant grow because it grew fifteen centimeters. I asked students to turn to their table partners and share weather they agreed or disagreed with this assertion and why. After a minute or two of debate, I cold called students to share out their conjecture. Many had determined that this evidence wouldn't address the hypothesis. They didn't know if the plant grew better or worse because they had nothing to compare it to. At this point, they pretty much guided themselves to the idea that they needed to have plants to which they did not apply the independent variable…"regular plants" as many of the students phrased it. Once they had the concept, we named it. Each team's experiment would need a control group.

Students worked in groups to further elaborate their experimental procedures. I coached them along the way, once again guiding them with questions to think about during their planning. In their Science Fair Journals, they had produced rough procedures with many formatting issues. However, they had enough to get going. They were ready and eager to begin.

We spent one day in class setting up the experiments. I had placed the materials in stations around the room and assigned roles for each member of the four person teams. As students followed through with their procedures step by step, I circulated around the room and asked questions, which threw wrenches into their works. When I saw them adding soil, I would ask "So, how much soil are you using?" This would prompt some re-thinking. "Ooops, we didn't measure." I'd remind them to record the results of this thinking in their Journals. I'd notice them doing something like breaking up clumps of soil. I'd say, "That's a great idea, is it in your procedure? Make sure you write it down so you don't forget that you did it."

They had really created skeletal procedures. Who could blame them? They'd been doing the "light" version of the scientific method for so long. I found it very easy to point out many moments throughout this lesson where they were doing something that they hadn't spelled out in their written procedure. I'd point it out through questioning and remind them to write it down. In doing this, the students gradually added muscle to the skeletons of their procedures. Once they'd finished setting up their experiments, I polled the class, "how many of you noticed that you did things while setting up your experiment that you had not written down in your procedure?" Every hand went up. Kind of a trick question, right? I'd primed them for this.

To conclude this portion of the project, students created final drafts of their procedures. In teams, they brainstormed all the things they did, that they hadn't specifically outlined in their procedures. They each recorded their brainstormed items in their Journals. As homework, I asked them to individually write up their procedure. I gave them the instructions to include every detail so that anyone could read their procedure and repeat it exactly as they had. I gave them a rubric so my expectations were very clear. I required students to type their procedures as a Google document. This would represent the first piece of their formal Science Fair paper. Later they'd copy and paste this procedure into that larger final Lab Report. When the procedures were all submitted, I assessed them using the rubric.

It would be several days before we saw any growth in the rye grass seeds. This was good, because we needed to pause and figure out exactly how we would collect data. They had written questions in the form "How does __ affect the growth of rye grass." The independent variable that they'd chosen went in the first blank. Now, we needed to decide what we meant by "growth" and how we'd measure it.

I asked students to brainstorm with their teams the things that would help us decide if the plants had grown better or worse with their independent variables applied. They came up with height, color, number of sprouts, days until first sprouts, survival rate, longevity and a few others. I used this list to explain and define "dependent variables." The dependent variables were the results of the experiment. These variables would depend on the trash item we added to the soil (which was the independent variable). A colleague of mine prefers using the term "responding variable," which more aptly describes the concept than "dependent variable." However, they'll be using the phrase "dependent variable" in math and science classes for many years to come, so why not get them ready for it?

Once we had a list of possible dependent variables, I led the students through creating a measurement protocol. Again, working in teams, students discussed and wrote down ways to measure each of the dependent variables they had come up with. Most groups offered using a ruler to measure the height. The also had ideas like counting the number of sprouts they could see, observing and describing the color, and keeping track of time by recording the date of each observation. Finally, as a class, we organized these ideas into a formal measurement protocol: a series of steps we'd follow each time we observed the plants.

With our plants germinating and our measurement protocol established, we now needed only to wait and measure. We'd measure and water the plants twice per week. This didn't take very much class time, so I decided that we'd delve into our formal Geology curriculum on Earth's History. On measurement days, we'd spend the first five minutes of class (the "Do Now") taking measurements and watering plants, and then move on with the curriculum.

I used the measurement time to push their thinking about data gathering. Some of their initial decisions from their procedures caused them difficulty at this point. For example, some teams had planted far too many seeds to sort through and measure now that the grass began growing. They problem solved and came up with ways to make better, more meaningful measurements. Some decided to measure the three tallest plants in each sprouter cell. Some decided to measure the shortest and tallest of each cell. Some tried to measure all the grass. Some of the students made measurement decisions that would not give them the data needed to draw conclusions about their hypothesis. This would become a very significant learning moment. More on that later.

After a few weeks of measuring, students had enough data to start their analysis. Off they went to math class. This was an awesome moment. For the second time those little blue exam books, their Science Fair journals, left their Science class and entered another. The students would actively use them in math. Taking this work from one class and using it to do work in another drove home the idea that students need skills from all their classes to complete a science experiment: it's interdisciplinary.

I met with the math teacher to determine the way students would work on their data analysis. The math teacher wanted to work on graphing. So she spent a few days with students teaching them to organize their data, and to choose among the different ways to represent it. They related what they knew, abstractly, about graphs and graphing to the data that they had generated in Science class. In the end, students had each produced a graph that they felt best represented their data along with a short discussion paragraph. The math teacher had assessed the work and entered the score into my big spreadsheet.

They returned to science class armed with their graphs and their ideas. I used this opportunity to teach them a new twenty-first century skill. I created a lesson where they entered their data into a Google spreadsheet, which they used to make an electronic version of their graph. Now they had another piece of their final Lab Report ready to cut and paste and a new skill they could use all the way through twelfth grade.

With data and graphs in hand, students had everything they needed to draw conclusions about their hypotheses. Off to Language Arts for some argumentative writing. Here is where I ran into a hitch. I'm going to elaborate on it a little to show that this whole project didn't go perfectly smoothly in my school. You may think, "I see how you were able to do this, but I can't because..." Lots went right for our new Science Fair idea. However, some things didn't go as planned, also.

When it came time for students to do their argumentative writing, I learned that they wouldn't be doing it in their Language Arts class. I was not expecting nor had I planned for this. Moreover, the deadline for completing Science Fair projects approached relentlessly. I could not put off my classroom Science Fair presentations because that would exclude my students from school-wide Science Fair. So I hustled to get my students' writing done in Science class. I created lessons, rubrics, assignment directions, power points, etc. I dedicated several class days for students to work. I signed out a cart of laptops. Was I able to get it done? Yes. Did I do as good a job at teaching argumentative writing as an experienced Language Arts teacher could? Certainly not, but I think I did an adequate job. You can, too, if need be. There's' more info on this in the Appendices.

You may experience times in Science Fair when things don't go as planned. In fact, it' almost preordained. It may make it harder to reach your goals, but some ingenuity and elbow grease will get you through it. This wrinkle may have made my Science Fair less than ideal, but it still represented a huge improvement over every other Science Fair I've run. Plus, students did end up doing some really cool work connected to Science Fair in their Language Arts class involving independent reading, connections to big picture global issues, and student created "stop-motion animations." This was a super-cool expansion of the whole ideas of what a Science Fair could be and made the work even more relevant to students' lives. However, that's a topic for another book.

In my lessons on using Science Fair data to engage in argumentative writing, I used what we call in my district the CER format. The writing took the form Claim, Evidence, Reasoning. To write the conclusion for their experiment, students made a claim about whether or not their hypothesis was supported by the evidence. They then stated the evidence for their claim. This involved a discussion of the data and parameters of the experiment. Finally, they explained how their evidence supported their claim. In other words, they connected the evidence to the claim.

At this point, many students ran into problems. Either during the data analysis, or as they contemplated writing their conclusions, they realized that they did not have sufficient data to support or refute their hypothesis. They had not captured robust data. Some had too many plants and their strategy to manage them didn't measure up. For example, one group had decided to measure their tallest and shortest plant in each cell and calculate an average. However, in some cases one or more of those measured plants died. Some had measured only the tallest and shortest plant of all the plants in all six cells! Upon analysis and with some coaching from me, they discovered that these measurements could not provide enough evidence to draw a conclusion. So how would they write their concluding paragraph?

Many students hastily concluded that their experiment failed or didn't work. I, however, recognized a huge opportunity for a teachable moment. As students stressed out about how they'd finish their project, I asked them to reflect on why the data they had collected couldn't help them assess their hypothesis. Every one of them could identify their particular flaw. They had invested so much in the experiment. They had created it from the ground up. They knew why each step of the procedure was there because they wrote it. So, they could easily spot the hole in their plan at this point. Moreover, as I pushed them to reflect further, they could also identify changes that would have provided the necessary evidence. One student asked me, "Mr. Shopis, can we start over, I want my experiment to be a success." I asked her what went wrong and she told me. I said, "You're experiment was a success, and what you just told me is your concluding paragraph." The fact that students could reflect upon and evaluate their work on that level was a HUGE win for them and me. This kind of thinking NEVER happened during traditional Science Fair for the great majority of students. In an ideal world, these reflections could lead to a second iteration of their experiments. However, for these seventh graders, this would have to wait until eighth grade.

Eventually, each student submitted one paragraph minimum. Some wrote conclusions that supported or refuted their hypotheses. Other submitted paragraphs that identified issues with their data and offered improvements for an imagined second round of tests. I assessed the writing using a rubric and I entered the scores on the big spreadsheet I'd developed for tallying their final grade. Once again, the students worked via Google docs so when it came time to assemble their final Lab Report they merely had to copy and paste all the pieces together.

Finally, with our data collected, graphs plotted, and conclusions drawn, we began the last part of the experiment: writing the Abstract. To do this each student needed to summarize his or her entire experience in two hundred and fifty words or less. Many students struggled to keep under this limit. In previous years, most students didn't come close to the limit. I think I owed this to the increased engagement and success with the scientific process that we created by doing Science Fair this new way. They simply had more to say because they grappled with the process more completely. They absorbed the process more. Students worked on their abstracts in class as well as for homework. I scored them with a rubric and added the scores to the spreadsheet.

With all the parts of their Lab Report done, students now assembled them together. To do this they created a new Google doc and copied and pasted all the pieces into it. Their reports began with their abstracts. Next, they inserted their background research. Then their question and hypothesis, etc. They submitted the reports to me via a website called turnitin.com. They didn't stress out over the lab report because they'd done all the work already and now merely assembled and submitted it.

At this point in the traditional Science Fair, teachers usually despair at the gigantic stack of papers they need to grade. Each paper required assessment and feedback. This would be an enormous burden on a teacher's time even if all the papers were very good. Add to that the frustration of so much time invested in low quality lab reports. However, this year I had a different experience. The papers were of much higher quality. Moreover, the heavy grading was done. I had graded each piece of the lab report as it came due. Now I just needed to make sure all the pieces were there and in the correct format. So I included one more column in the spreadsheet that tallied all the parts of their project. This column represented a score for submitting a complete lab report. I did a simple scan through each paper to make sure students had included all the parts and the grading was done.

For the next phase of Science Fair, students created their presentations. In a traditional fair, each would get a tri-fold board and paste all the components of the project to it. The endeavor would conclude with them setting up their board and waiting to be judged/graded on Fair day. Instead of this, we had an electronic Science Fair. Students worked in their teams of four to create a Google slide show and oral presentation. I gave them criteria for the presentations and some class time to work together. Since they created presentations using their Google drives, they could collaborate on a shared slide show and work together virtually when they were at home. Each day they worked, I had them spend the last five minutes of class reflecting on what they needed to get done before the next class and assign it to themselves as homework. They recorded this assignment like a regular homework so they could hold each other accountable the next day.

When they completed their work, we had our Science Fair day in class. Each group had five minutes to give their presentations. I had given them the rubric I'd use to grade them. I used our "Whole School Verbal Communication Rubric." This tied our Science Fair to some of our school goals. I advised them to plan on each member using one minute so if they went over a little they'd still finish in the allotted time. I also explained that each student would be graded individually base on the portion of the presentation that they gave. I'd created a spreadsheet using the grading rubric that allowed me to grade the students on-the-fly as they gave their presentations. I also gave a comment sheet to all the students in the class. Their assignment for that day was to assess each presentation they saw. With each team taking five minutes to present and seven teams per class, we could finish in thirty-five minutes plus transition time. Our science Fair presentations easily fit into one class period of forty-seven minutes. When class ended, so did Science Fair and the grading was done.

In my school, we have a school-wide Science Fair. Each science teacher can choose up to two students per class to participate. I chose my students by looking at their lab report grade and their presentation grade. The two students in each class with the highest grades went on to compete in the school-wide Science Fair. I coached these few students through making a tri-fold board. We did this during study halls and after school. This wasn't very hard for the kids. They'd done all the hard work. At that point, they just needed to format it for display on the boards. So, in a few days my Science Fair "winners" had prepared themselves to compete in the school-wide fair. For me, this represented the end of Science Fair for this year.

12. Saving Science Fair in Your Whole School

If you've read this far, you probably buy into the premise of this approach to Science Fair. You're ready to let go of some of the Science Fair sacred cows like each student having a unique topic and you're comfortable with teaching process over content. You're ready to teach Science Fair like you'd teach any other topic. You're ready to treat Science Fair like a curriculum instead of a project. I did these things and it greatly increased the amount of student learning and reduced my frustration with the whole process. I saved my Science Fair.

However, if you're ready to do all this you can do more than save Science Fair in your classroom. You can save Science Fair in your whole school. You can scale up what you've done in your class. This will be harder because it requires more teachers to buy-in and more coordination. You may also need to do some convincing with your principal. However, if your principal values student learning over the flashiness of traditional Science Fair you should be able to make the case.

You can scale up Science Fair in your school by adding more freedom and accountability as students get older. After a few years, students will have had a few very guided experiences to use as exemplars. As they digest more of the scientific process, they can become more independent with it.

Use Google drive to assist with this. If you have students do all their work on their Google drives, they will have a year-by-year portfolio of the projects they've done. They can then refer back when doing a new project. Therefore, if they find themselves wondering how to complete one portion of the project they can always ask themselves, "Well, how did I do that last year" and check out previous years' work.

Each year's work can form the basis of the following year's project. If a teacher knows that all the students in front of them have a project on their Google drive they can use it as a starting point. Student can begin the whole Science Fair process for the year by revisiting their project from last year on their Google drive and reflecting on it. A new project could then be a second iteration of the previous year's project. For example, if their data was insufficient to address their hypothesis, they could redesign the experiment and try again. This actually represents authentic science.

Alternatively, they can perform a variation of the previous year's experiment. They could do the same experiment, but change up the variables. In the case of my Science Fair, their eighth grade teacher could have them see if their conclusions apply to other species of grass or to other plants altogether. If some of the students had puzzling results from the previous year, you could base this year's project on experiments designed to explain them. Indeed, students could engage in many options using a previous year's experiment as the basis for a new experiment.

You could also redesign a new Science Fair experience based on different curricular goals. Make Science Fair work for you and your students. You have goals for the content and skills students must learn. Wrap Science Fair in those goals. Using our rye grass experiment as an example, perhaps the eighth grade teacher has new observation and measurement tools that students will learn to use. Part of their Science Fair could be the incorporation of these tools. For example, if a teacher wants students to be able to use a microscope to make detailed observations, then do that with the grass. Students could look at root tips of experimental and control plants, sketch them and elaborate on differences. They could also look at the blades. Do they see more or fewer chloroplasts in the cells of the experimental grass? Do they observe differences in stomates? Do they see any other differences on the cellular level? Bacteria? Fungi? Clearly, by repeating an experiment, students could have the opportunity to apply lots of skills and content that derives from your state's science standards.

Each year as students get more of a grip on the process of doing science, the content can become more relevant. When the process isn't so hard, the content can be. Alternatively, instead of ramping up the content expectations, you could push harder and harder on the process. Students' science skills could go deeper as the process of Science Fair becomes more and clearer to them. You could increase what the students must do in order to meet your expectations for each part of the project: the hypothesis, procedure, etc…

By the time students reach the upper grades, they'll have several years' projects under their belts. They'll be ready to take on more responsibility and independence with their Science Fair projects. If you're a high school teacher, now you can go about Science Fair in two ways. First, keep making it work for you. Assign projects on kinetic energy, cells, bacterial reproduction, rates of reaction, etc… Merge it with your content. Ideally students will have the process down, so they can engage in content that is more relevant.

Moreover, you can increase your expectations about their content findings. For my middle school students, nobody really cared if adding pencil shavings to soil helped their grass grow. In fact, the complexities of testing such a variable in a valid, manner were much too great for an introductory experiment. There are so many variables in a classroom setting that cannot be controlled. Even if students discerned a difference in their control and experimental plants, it would be highly questionable that their variable caused the difference. That wasn't the point, though. The point was to start them on a path of scientific thinking. I let go of content. We focused on process.

After years of this, though, a high school teacher can begin to focus on content. Students will have built the skills over their years of Science Fair to propose and carry out experiments that could lead them to relevant content. Students can use their Science Fair skills to learn new, standards based science. Also, wouldn't it be interesting for a Senior to look back at their seventh grade project on their Google drive and critique it? Perhaps revise it? Their new, process honed eyes might see those old projects in a whole new way.

Instead of assigning content specific projects, however, you could also give the students complete independence. Now Science Fair can be a project instead of a whole curriculum. Older high school students no longer need every step of the process scaffolded like they did in seventh grade. Moreover, they have a whole Google drive of projects to draw from and to use as exemplars. You can target your assessment on whatever aspects of the scientific process you wish to emphasize. In this new version of Science Fair, students can actually arrive at a point in the upper grades that most of us (unfairly) expect them to perform at in middle school and sometimes even in elementary school!

Epilogue: Dividends

Later That Same Year

My students were at a point in Science Fair where they'd already submitted their procedures. They'd used them to set up their rye grass projects and had time to revise and submit them. Now they engaged in a non-Science Fair lesson on Geology. We were investigating limestone and one of its ingredients: Calcite. We had brainstormed, as a class, what the source of the calcite found in this rock might be.

Once we had a list of possible sources of Calcite, I supplied them with materials, and teams of students created a plan for finding out the real source. They discussed the problem in teams and came up with a procedure to test out a variety of sources for Calcite.

As they brainstormed in teams and worked out their plans, I circulated around the room. I checked in and coached the teams as they worked. To my great surprise and delight, students wrote up their procedures in their notebooks in the format we'd used for their Science Fair procedures. Moreover, they asked questions that reflected their learning during Science Fair. "Mr. Shopis, should I be writing down the number of drops of Hydrochloric Acid we want to use in my procedure?" "Mr. Shopis, do I use the same number of drops on every material?" "Should we create a table to record our results?" "What's the independent variable in this experiment?"

Students put much more effort into their procedures. Consequently, the procedures were much more robust. Normally, students put very rough effort into their procedures. They were a means to an end. If I saw that their plan would provide them with the observations necessary to make the content connections, I'd move them along. Plans had always been rough, poorly formatted, and lacked rigor in terms of process. In the past, "It was the content, stupid."

However, now their questions reflected a new way of thinking about the process of Science. They still strove for the same content objective on the topic of Geology. However, they also embraced process as well. As they worked, they not only learned factual information about rocks, but also applied the process skills they'd developed during Science Fair. They were doing Science. Formal Science. Not just an activity, but an experiment. The students themselves transformed their typical class inquiry experience from "process-light" into real Scientific investigation. I noticed for the first time in twelve years that Science Fair helped make Science a verb.

***

I anticipate that this endeavor will continue to pay dividends over the course of these students' academic careers. If my school scales up the efforts we made in seventh grade all the way up to twelfth, then the investment will pay off many times more. By the time my crop of seventh graders embark on their senior year, they may very well have the tools to take on a legitimate independent scientific research experiment.

Moreover, teaching students science skills may take the sting out of Science electives. With a host of new process skills acquired during their middle and early high school years, they will see Science Fair as just another part of Science class. They'll stop seeing it as this monster they must fight every year. It's a fight they usually lose. Now, it's just an assignment. Hopefully, with this new outlook students will no longer shy away from Science electives. They'll take that biomedical research class because it looks cool and won't think twice if someone tells them they'll have to do a Science Fair project.

One year in my school, a group of science teachers and I dreamed up an upper class elective which basically amounted to a Science Fair class. Students would show up in the lab each day and work on their own scientific research. The teacher would assist students in this research by individually coaching the students through the process and offering whole class lessons as needed. Kids could do a few iterations of the process throughout the year. We imagined that the real Science Fair rock stars would sign up for this class. Kids from this class would go on to be super-prepared for college level Science work. If students had the skills, acquired through years of formal teaching of Science Fair, this dream might work!

These ideas would require a lot of work by a lot of people beyond my seventh grade classroom. The whole Science team would have to get behind the ideological shift in Science Fair (It's a curriculum, not a project!). Administrators in the building would need to sign off. New Science Fair curricula would have to be designed across grade levels and vertically aligned so that what students did in one grade prepared them for what they'd do in the next. We have the luxury in our school of containing a grade span from seventh through twelfth grade. This makes it easier but not easy.

Big plans start from little things. This year my seventh grade partner and I changed Science Fair in our classrooms because we were tired of investing so much time and effort into something that had so little payoff for students. We followed the basic philosophy of "it's a curriculum, not a project" so we taught it like that. We let go of a lot of Science Fair sacred cows. We brought the project into our classrooms instead of students' homes. We taught everyone the same thing. Each student did a variation of the same project. Students learned collaboratively in teams of four, just like they did for all their science learning. In the end, we worked very hard. However, the work had purpose and achieved goals. It made students stronger science learners instead of scaring them off with frustration and failure. It prepared them to not just learn Science, but to do Science. It created the opportunity for our whole school to transform our teaching of Science process. These changes could help our students become real Science thinkers and participants in the twenty-first century economy.

Science Fair doesn't have to suck. Use what I've outlined in this book or just take the pieces of it that will fit in your classroom. Keep the big picture in mind and make it work for your students. Make Science Fair a real learning opportunity for your kids. You can stop banging your head against the wall and start seeing results for all your hard Science Fair work. Give it a shot for a year. Afterward, you might find yourself thinking for the first time, "Congratulations on an excellent Science Fair."

Acknowledgements

It's hard to imagine making changes in a school without many people involved. I'm fortunate enough to have really great teachers and administrators with whom I worked alongside to change our Science Fair program in our seventh grade. Education is a collaborative endeavor. While one teacher can do great things within the confines of his or her four walls, so much of what we do is begged, borrowed, or stolen from peers and those that came before us.

In that light, the core of my little band of thieves, the "science squad," consisted of two teachers and our Program Director. First, none of the changes would have been possible without the amazing Gloria Restrepo. We dreamed this whole idea up together. Everything I did for my five sections of science classes, she did for another five. Our Science Program Director, Liz Baker helped us brainstorm and supported our changes to Science Fair all along the way. I can't imagine having accomplished what we did without a leader who recognized good teaching and was so supportive of positive change.

I also work on a seventh grade team of awesome, collaboration-minded teachers, all of whom played a role in Science Fair this year. Thanks to the energetic Lillie Marshall, for listening to my ideas and welcoming those little blue Science Fair journals into her room for student background research. Thanks also to Tu Vu for working with kids to crunch their Science Fair data and adding still more to the blue books. It took us a while, but our ever-positive Latin teacher, Donna Markis, discovered a way to bring Science Fair into her curriculum, putting her imprint on the blue Science Fair journals. A huge thanks goes to the unflappable English Language Arts teacher Cathy O'Flaherty who not only leads our team, but brought Science Fair to a whole new level by expanding it and building a huge amount of learning around it in her classroom. Co-forging our seventh grade interdisciplinary curriculum was ELA teacher Kellyanne Mahoney. She burned some serious midnight oil creating a Science Fair independent reading list and a host of other Science Fair activities for her ELA students. Her efforts never fail to inspire me. Finally, I'd like to thank my Headmaster, Emilia Pastor, who has always supported me in all my classroom endeavors.

I owe a lot to many others in my school for support throughout the year on matters other than Science Fair. Tracy Wagner, whose proximity to my classroom frequently results in short visits from me for support, has never failed to provide it. I have also greatly enjoyed tossing ideas around with and pondering our "oddballness" with math teacher Sean Moran.

My experience with Science Fair has been a twelve-year saga. Along the way, I've collaborated (co-conspired) with several educators. First and foremost, I'd like to thank Bob Ettinger. We've spent huge amounts of time trying to figure out Science Fair and countless hours conspiring on every imaginable aspect of Science teaching. In addition, the hardest working person in the world, Pam Pelletier, Director of Science for Boston Public Schools, has always completely supported science teachers and totally gets what we go through at Science Fair time.

Old friends sometimes help out in new ways. My childhood friend-turned-scientist, Joe Jankovsky took days off work, and patiently tolerated my early efforts at Science Fair as a judge.

I'd be remiss if I failed to mention two of my biggest influences as a science teacher. My mom, Nicolina Shopis recently retired from her career as a middle school science teacher. Her mentorship, especially in my first years teaching, helped carry me through. She still coaches and inspires me. As a child, I spent immeasurable hours and years contemplating the secrets of the universe with my dad, Jorge Shopis. He always fanned the embers of my curiosity and guided me through the highs and lows of life.

My biggest booster in all my endeavors from switching careers in order to become a teacher, to taking time to write a book, has been my incredible wife, Mia Shopis. She continues to nurture the dreamer in me and helps me hang onto a small piece of the little boy who used look up at the sky and say, wow!

Appendices

The appendices contain an array of resources for you to use in your classroom. There are lessons, "sheets" for students, rubrics and other documents. I am including downloadable versions on my web site at **www.sciencenugget.com/resources.** There are PDF as well as MS Word versions of all the resources.

In addition, I have also made the resources in the appendices available in my Google drive. You will find them at **http://tinyurl.com/ mbuha2u**. Going to the link will bring you to a folder of Google documents and PDFs. You'll need a gmail account to view the Google drive documents. Creating one is simple and free

The formatting of the documents (especially the rubrics) will be much easier to read in either of these web locations than they are in this book. Please feel free to download and customize any documents you wish.

Appendix A: Lessons

Lesson 1: Introduction

Group the students
- I had students work in teams of four. Each team set up one six-pack seed sprouter. The decisions were made as a team. However, each team was further divided into pairs. So, once the experiment was set up and running, each pair was responsible for taking and recording its own data with the plants. Later, when it came time to write reports and give presentations. Each individual student submitted their own report, and teams gave presentations. The grouping was very fluid as teams of four would break into pairs for some work and then team back up for other activities. I tried to be flexible about this. Sometimes it just worked better to have four heads thinking through an issue and at other times fewer voices was more efficient.

Introduce project with sheet
- I distributed the "Introduction" sheet (See Appendix B) to the students and gave them a few minutes to read over it silently. At this point, there are a number of things you can do to emphasize the major points. Have them "turn and talk" with a partner and describe two major points from the intro sheet. Lead a whole class discussion. Generate a list of student questions to address based on what they read. The point is to drive home the idea that the whole human food chain depends on grass. So, a minor discovery about grass growth can have a big impact on how we eat. This will set the stage for the whole project.

Set up lab notebooks
- I purchased a bulk set of small blue exam books and charged students one dollar for each one. This covered the cost of the

books and all the materials I bought for the project. I bought the blue books on amazon.com. See the "Resources" page at the end of this book for more info.

- In class, students set up their lab notebooks with their names, and any other relevant identifying information. I also included the names of their teammates, and section number. All this was included on the cover. The booklets only have sixteen pages, so we worked efficiently.

- These booklets were the heart of the experiment. All data will be recorded there, as well as ideas, questions, aha's, etc.

Review rules and purpose of lab notebook.

- I had two basic rules for the lab notebook. Rule #1: Never erase. The purpose of this rule is to maintain data integrity. This is not a huge issue with seventh grade projects; however, in the grown-up science world it is very important. Erasures in lab notebooks introduce uncertainty into the validity of data. To insure validity, errors are crossed out with one line. This way anyone reading the notebook can see what the error was and that it was, in fact, innocent and not of malicious intent. Getting students into this habit now will make it automatic as they advance in their science education.

- Rule #2: Date every entry. This allows students to review their data and orient it chronologically. Moreover, the dates on the page can become data itself, showing intervals between spurts of growth or general longevity of the plants. It also helped me to guide students back through their experiment to discover where problems were introduced.

Begin Using the Lab Notebook

- The first entry into the notebook will be the first homework assignment. They'll brainstorm a list of waste items that their family normally throws away, but might be used to improve the growth of grass.

Homework: *Brainstorm a list of at least three waste items that your family normally throws away that might be used to help grass grow.*

Lesson 2: Choose an Independent Variable and Write the Question

Share trash items from homework
- At the beginning of class, ask students to volunteer the trash items from their list. As they rattle off their items, create a big class list on the board. I use a video projector to project a word processing document on which I record all suggestions. This creates a long list of potential items. Doing it electronically allows me to save it as a document to bring back later. You can also accomplish this in a more low-tech fashion with chart paper.

Teams Choose Their Item
- With the big class list displayed, have students team up in their groups of four and select one item from the list to test out. My teams debated this for five minutes or so, and almost all of them came to consensus on their own. Some needed a little nudging. Asking students why they thought their choice would be the best to test could help identify which students had some relevant knowledge and which were being a bit stubborn. Some teams thought of innovative ways to test more than one.

Introduce the question format
- There are several question formats to use when doing a science experiment. The two I've used in the past are:

  - If change _____ what will happen to _____ *or*

  - How does _____ affect _____

- For this project, I used the second. However, the first may be better for nascent science experimenters as it more explicitly indicates the independent variable as the one the scientist manipulates. Once the students have been introduced to the question format, they need to write the question in their notebooks. My students wrote questions like: How do used coffee grounds affect the growth of grass, and How do pencil shavings affect the growth of grass. (I gave them the words to fill into the last blank; they merely had to insert their chosen trash item in the first blank).

- When I did this, I was surprised by some of the question forms that students wrote. Despite the fact that I'd given them the format with only one blank to fill in, they still strayed from the formula. It was a good exercise for me to cruise the room as they and their partners wrote their questions and provide on-the-spot feedback. Some incorporated different question forms from previous experiences. Others didn't quiet grasp what we were getting at for some reason. A little coaching helped this along.

Identify the independent and dependent variables

- With their question written, it's time to introduce them to independent and dependent variables. In previous iterations of Science Fair, I'd tried to teach variables before I introduced the question format. However, I found it easier to teach about variables once the question was written. This way, we were taking apart the question and analyzing it rather than building it up from scratch. Once we've seen a question and what its guts look like, students will be able to construct one of their own better in the future.

- I tell the students that in Science experiments there are two types of variables. One variable the scientist chooses and changes. The other variable happens on its own and the scientist measures. I displayed a sample question from a volunteer and asked students to debate which were the two variables and then predict which they thought was which. They conducted this debate in pairs. I then had the pairs team up into their groups of four and continue the debate. Finally, I cold called students to report their ideas with a justification. Sometimes there was near unanimity about which was the independent and which was the dependent variable. However, sometimes the report-out led to vigorous argument. Repeating the process for another example might be in order for increased practice. By the end of the discussion students annotate their own questions in their lab notebooks by underlining their two variables and labeling one "independent variable" and the other "dependent variable."

Lessons 3 & 4: Background Research

Hand-off to Humanities

- Explain that they'll make a hypothesis next, but first they need to learn more about their topic. Researching their topic will help them make a more informed hypothesis. To get more info on their topic, they'll do library or internet research. At this point in our Science Fair, they brought their blue Science Fair notebooks into their Humanities (Social Studies) class to learn about research methods and visit the library. I found this a powerful moment in the process as it broke down the walls between disciplines and showed them that Science experimentation is an inherently interdisciplinary endeavor. They will, indeed, need to use their learning from all their classes to complete a successful experiment. To this end, they'll do library and internet research in Humanities.
- The tack that our humanities teacher took was identifying valid resources on the Internet and correct sourcing. These were topics she was going to teach anyway. She just used Science Fair as the vehicle. She spent a total of 2 class days on this.

- She had students brainstorm as list of ten questions whose answers would help them predict the outcome of their experiment. Once the students had their lists, they chose two questions to research. They did this research in the library using books and internet resources. Most of their research ended up being from the internet. She addressed with them what constituted a valid internet resource.
- By the end of the process, students had written a summary paragraph for what they'd discovered about each of their two questions. Many of them found information on photosynthesis and a variety of soil nutrients such as calcium, phosphorus, nitrogen, etc. Others uncovered information about decomposition and its role in soil development. Some of the students' research was directly relevant to their Science Fair questions. Some was not. However, now they had a wealth of information to attempt to apply to the writing of a hypothesis. They recorded all of this in their blue Science Fair notebook.

Lesson 5: Hypotheses

Introduce Hypothesis
- Students return to Science Class with heir blue Science Fair notebooks to put their research to use in their experiments.
- Begin class by showing students the Hypothesis format. I use a specific format for writing hypotheses. If_____, then_____ because_____. I use this format because it forces students to think about the reasons for their predictions. Moreover, if correctly implemented, it also contains the seed of the entire experimental procedure.

Use exemplar to explain it
- I like to show students at least one exemplar to use as a model.

There are several at sciencebuddies.com. I used this exemplar:

- **If** dry bread and moist bread are left in bags for two weeks, **then** the moist bread will grow mold more quickly **because** mold is a living organism and organisms need water to survive.

- As you can see, the basic experimental setup is contained within the hypothesis. Moreover, their "because" contains their research based reasoning.

Have students write a rough hypothesis in their Science Fair journal

- Once students have the format for the Hypothesis down, have them write a rough hypothesis for their own experiment in their journal. For example: "If some soil is mixed with crushed egg shells, then the seeds planted in the soil with egg shells will grow taller because egg shells contain calcium which is a nutrient that plants need. This is an actual hypothesis written by one of my students. It's a bit clunky but you can see that the whole idea for the experiment is contained within the hypothesis. Moreover, requiring the "because" has allowed the student to explain how their research informed their hypothesis.

Debate Hypotheses

- The teams of four (who all have selected the same independent variable) then debate their hypotheses. Their debates should be informed by the research they did. Since each student researched their own two questions, they should have a wealth of material for debate.

Attempt to arrive at consensus

- Ideally, students should arrive at some consensus for a hypothesis. However, this is not required. After all, they'll be gathering data that will ideally settle their debate by the end of the experiment.

Re-write Hypotheses

- After they've share, debated, and amended their hypotheses, they should re-write it in their journals. This version should be based on their discussion and debate and will represent their final hypothesis upon which they'll base their experimental procedure.

Lesson 6: Procedures

Groups brainstorm plan to test hypotheses

- In teams of four, students brainstorm a plan to test their hypotheses. They should not yet write their rough ideas in their journals.
- Have students report out on their ideas to the class. After going over a few ideas, you should be hearing some version of the following: applying the variable (trash) to a plant and seeing how it grows. If the students don't come up with the idea of a control plant (a plant without the variable applied) here's the place to introduce it. If students simply say to apply their chosen variable and see if it grows better, ask them "how will you know if it grows better?" Use this question as a basis for discussion about planting a seed without the variable for comparison. I usually have students think on this in pairs or teams of four.

Show them the materials

- Once the students have a rough idea of a procedure, show them the materials they will have available. I find that in many cases, showing them the materials ahead of time limits or influences their thinking. Sometimes this makes it harder for them to wrap their minds around the question because they move right into wanting to build stuff with the materials.
- After students have settle on the basic idea, tell them they will have the following materials to make it work:

- 1 six-pack seed sprouter for each team of four.
- Winter rye grass seeds.
- Soil
- Water
- Graduated Cylinder
- Pipettes
- Their trash item
- Sticker dots for labeling
- Rulers
- Hand lenses
- Any other materials you may wish to supply them with

Re-plan with specific materials in mind

- Now students make a more specific plan using the materials available to them. They should discuss exactly what they'll do to grow and collect data on their plants. Cruise the room and guide their thinking. When they've got a good idea going, they should write the procedure in their blue Science Fair notebooks along with a materials list.
- This will be the first draft of their procedure. Of course, it will be incomplete and lack required specificity. It's hard to foresee all the little things that come up when setting up an experiment. Don't worry; they'll take another pass at it later.
- See Appendix C for a rubric to assess procedures.

Lesson 7: Experimental Setup

Follow Procedures

- On this day students follow their plan and set up their experiment. I have the materials available at stations around the room. Water is at one station, soil at another, etc. Students send one member of their team to get the stuff they need. I only allow them to use items from their materials list. If they need an additional item, they must add it to their list.

- Circulate around the room and offer guidance and coaching. It's particularly important to point out when students do something that's not in their procedure. For example, many students had the step "add soil" in their procedure, but ended up measuring a specific amount. I'd ask them if the measuring was part of their procedure and told them they should write it in. Some teams also broke up the clumps of soil. I told them to add that step to the procedure. Students began to see that they actually did a lot more than was written in their procedures.

- While circulating I also emphasized the need to measure things. I'd ask questions like "how much water are you going to add," or "how many seeds will you plant in each sprouter cell?"

Reflect on setup and revise procedures

- After their grass is planted and labeled, have students reflect on their experimental set-ups and revise their procedures. Emphasize that their procedures should contain everything that they did. They should be detailed enough so that anyone could read their procedure and repeat their experiment.

Homework: *Write final draft of procedure as a Google doc and submit it on turnitin.com.*

I gave students a rubric for how I would grade their procedures. Their assignment was to write the final draft of their procedures and turn it in to me for a grade. I had students type it up as a Google doc and use turnitin.com to submit the assignment. It has a great rubric feature that makes assessment a lot easier. Plus, then the students have a permanent record of their final procedure.

Lesson 8: Observation Protocol

Distribute sprouters to groups
- After one day, their sprouters should show no growth. Use this time to generate an observation protocol with them.
- They will figure out how and what to measure to determine if their hypotheses are correct.

Revisit question
- Have students open their blue Science Fair notebooks and re-read their original question "How does _____ affect the growth of grass." Review the idea of "dependent variable." In this case it's "growth."

Brainstorm measurements
- In groups of four, have students brainstorm ways they could measure growth. As they report out, make a big list on the board. Some of the items will be easy to measure; others will be more difficult or require too much time. Our list looked like this:
    - Height
    - # of sprouts
    - Color
    - Days to first sprout
    - How long they live
    - Width of blades

Create class measurement protocol
- Use this list to create a measurement protocol for the students to use each time they check their plants. The protocol should be as specific as possible, but refrain from making too many suggestions on your own. Sometimes students realize later that their protocol is tricky to implement. For example if they wish to measure the height, they will quickly find that each cell

containing multiple seeds has sprouts of different heights. I find that these moments are often the best learning opportunities as students debate the best way to represent the height. Some will measure each sprout and take an average. Some will decide to measure the tallest and shortest in each cell.

- In some cases, the decisions students make will not lead them to collecting sufficient data to either support or refute their hypothesis. This is okay, because they will have ample material to reflect upon in order to describe where they went awry later on. If they can pinpoint exactly why they have insufficient data and how they would rework their experiment to solve those problems, then they really have learned. So coach them, but don't go overboard. Failure is a requirement of science. If they're basing everything on their own ideas and reasoning, even if they're flawed, they'll have a really good shot at fixing it later.

Include steps on watering

- It's important that students water their plants. The seed sprouters hold a limited amount of water that evaporates rather quickly. I had students check their plants every two to three days. Each time they made measurements, they also watered their plants. Make sure their protocols include steps on watering.

Lesson 9: Data Collection

Collect Data on the Back Burner

- At this point in the process, I moved on to another unit in Science Class. I did this because the measurements would only be taken every two to three days and would only take five to ten minutes of class time. The first day of taking measurements may take longer, but once it becomes routine, the students get through it pretty quick.
- Revise Protocols

- So, every 2-3 days spend first 5-10 minutes of class applying the measurement protocol. Coach students as they encounter issues. (i.e. too many seed sprouts, etc.). As you circulate through the room, push them to adjust their measurement protocol to address problems they encounter. They should include new steps for their protocol in their Science Fair journals.

Lesson 10-12: Data Analysis

Involve the Math Teacher
- Once data is collected and the students have recorded it all in their Science Fair notebooks, it's time for analysis. In my school, they took their blue books into math class for this portion of the project. This was another powerful moment in the process where the barriers between disciplines came down. They would do work that is totally normal for a math class, however the numbers they used had greater significance and meaning to them because the students generated the numbers themselves. They were not abstractions. They were numeric representations of the little green living things that the kids had cared for over the past few weeks.
- The math teacher focused her lessons on choosing the best type of graph to represent the data they'd collected. The students made a rough draft of a graph and then a final draft based on her feedback. She also had them write an analytic paragraph about the data and what it meant. When they returned to me after three days in math, they had final drafts of graphs with analytic writing.

Lesson 13: e-graphs

Introduce Google spread sheets

- Although the graphs that they'd created in math were excellent and had served the dual purpose of teaching ways to represent data as well as Science Fair data analysis, I also wanted their graphs in electronic form. There are a couple of ways to do this. One would be to scan their paper graphs or take a picture with your phone. However, I had students create graphs using Google spreadsheets. I spent a lesson modeling how to do it and then gave students class time to work on their own graphs. At my school, we have a cart of chrome books for these types of lessons. Your use of technology will depend entirely upon availability in your school and your own comfort level.

- Students work on their graphs and insert them into Google docs along with their analyses. I allowed students to complete the Google doc for homework. The assignment had already been graded by the math teacher. This grade would later become part of the total Science Fair project grade (along with the research grade from humanities and all the other portions done in science.)

Homework: Finish e-Graphs

Lesson 14: Conclusion Writing

Introduce Conclusion format

- With data in hand, students are ready to determine if it supports or refutes their initial hypothesis. At this time, introduce them to the format their conclusion should take. I have them write a one-paragraph conclusion. It should have three parts: 1. What were you trying to find out? 2. What you found out. 3. How you know. That's the basics of it. I try to steer students away from stating if their hypothesis is correct or not. Instead I have them state whether or not the evidence supports of refutes their hypothesis.

- See Appendices D and E for directions and rubric
- Students work on drafts of their concluding paragraphs in class. Circulate and support them as they work.

Homework: *Finish conclusions as a Google doc and upload to turnitin.com*

Lesson 15: Abstract Writing

Introduce Abstract
- At this point the project is done and conclusions drawn. To finish off their Science Fair paper, they'll need to write an abstract. In this lesson, I introduce the abstract as a summary for the entire project. They can write it in one paragraph and it should be no more than two hundred and fifty words.
- See Appendices F & G for directions and rubric.
- After a brief summary of the assignment and distributing the directions, hold a short Q&A to clarify directions and allow students to work. Circulate and support as they do their writing.

Homework: *finish abstracts as a Google doc and upload to turnitin.com*

Lesson 16: Assembling the paper

Introduce scope of assignment
- This is the last step of their Science Fair paper. If you had students create all the little pieces as Google docs, there's a big payoff here. Students will now copy and paste all the individual

parts of the experiment onto one document. Everything should be in its proper place. There's no additional work for students to generate. They're just assembling what they've done into one document.

- If you had students do all the work on paper, a little strategic planning ahead of time could result in just stapling together the different pages now. Otherwise, you can have them re-write all the pieces into a single paper.
- If you had them do all the components electronically, then the students merely need to cut and paste everything into one final document.
- See Appendix H for directions.

Work on assembly

- The class format runs the same as the previous two lessons. Summarize the assignment. Distribute the directions. After students read, allow some time for clarification Q&A. Students then work on the assembly. Circulate and support.

Homework: *Finish assembling the paper as a Google doc and upload it to turnitin.com*

Lesson 17: Google Presentations

Model Google Presentation

- Unlike the traditional Science Fair where all the work goes onto a tri-fold board, I had students create Google presentations: an e-Science Fair, if you will. I spent the beginning of this lesson modeling how to create a Google presentation. I projected my Google documents page and went through the steps of creating a new file and adding text and pictures. My students turned out to be pretty savvy at this.
- Don't feel limited, however, if you don't have access to the

technology for this. Go ahead and crate a presentation method that works for you. You can even go the old-school tri-fold board route.

Distribute assignment

- Then, like in the previous lessons, I distributed directions and coached them as they worked. The benefit of using a Google presentation, is that it made collaboration in a team of four very easy. They could create one Google presentation and "share" it amongst the team members. This way they could divide up the work and all contribute to the document simultaneously.
- I emphasized that students would be graded individually based on their participation in the presentation. Therefore, it behooved them to make a significant contribution.
- See Appendices I and K for directions and rubric.

Lesson 18: Oral presentation

Introduce oral presentations

- In this lesson, students create an oral presentation to go along with their Google presentations. These are the things that each member of the team will say as they go through their Google slides. It's important to emphasize that each student should participate equally and will be graded individually.
- After describing the assignment, distribute directions and hold a short clarification Q&A.
- As students work, circulate and support.
- See Appendices J and K for directions and rubric

Lesson 19: Finish and practice oral presentations

Work on presentations
- Students continue working on oral presentations. I provided index cards for them to jot notes. When they finished, most teams had time to practice. I had them give presentations to another team. This allowed students to tweak the timing and make sure they didn't go too long.

Lesson 20: Science Fair Day

Everyone participates
- During the oral presentations, every student took part in the judging. It was a requirement that each student filled out an evaluation sheet from each presentation he or she observed. I distributed evaluation sheets for them to record their scores on. This was a graded assignment. I gave students a chance to review them and ask questions.
- See Appendix L for evaluation sheet

Presentation time
- Students give their presentations in groups of four. You can change this around to suit your needs. Groups of two or even individual presentations may work better for you. Keep time for each presentation or appoint a student timekeeper. It's a good idea to give a thirty-second warning. I had a red card that I held up when there were thirty seconds left. I was pretty strict about cutting them off at five minutes. Not many groups went over the time.
- As you watch each presentation, you'll need to assess the students. It's difficult to remember after all the presentations are done, so I recommend doing it on the fly. I created a spreadsheet to record scores as the students presented that I

filled in as they went along. It's included in the resources for this book. You can also print out a score sheet if you're off line in school and just fill that in.

Conclusion:

That's an outline of the whole process as we did it at my school. You may choose to follow it pretty closely or pick it apart and use what works for you. The main idea here is to teach Science Fair like you'd teach any other topic. When you do it that way, all the great strategies and skills you've developed as a science teacher can be applied to Science Fair.

If your access to or comfort with electronic resources like Google docs and turnitin.com are limited, then definitely go analog. Everything I did "in the cloud" could be accomplished with pencil and paper. I just used those resources to make it work a little easier for me. Moreover, you may not have the level of coordination or buy-in from your teaching team to collaborate with the other disciplines in your grade. This is unfortunate. Who better to teach math concepts to students but a skilled and experienced math teacher! Likewise with Language Arts and Humanities. This makes it harder but still infinitely more beneficial to students. You may not be as skilled at teaching math as your math teacher may, but that's not the point. Remember, the real benefit of this method is not in the nitty gritty details but in the overall approach. Bring the project into school instead of home. Have students work on a variation of the same project. Teach Science Fair the same way you teach Science. Stop pulling your hair out and start teaching!

Appendix B: Intro Sheet for Students

Interdisciplinary Science Fair
Using Waste to Make a Better World

Introduction:
Can you use stuff that you normally just throw away to change the whole world? This year you will engage on a long-term science investigation that will require you to apply skills and knowledge from all of your classes. What you find out, may impact everyone, everywhere.

Topic: *Grass growth*
Grass. It's everywhere. It's so common that we usually don't even notice when it's there. However, grass is the foundation of the food chain for humans all over the planet Earth. Wheat, corn, and rice (all grasses) form a major portion of the food supply for most of the world. Moreover, cattle and other meat sources are fed mostly grass products as they grow. Without grasses, there is no food.

You will be investigating ways to re-use household wastes in order to improve the growth of grass. You will go through all the steps of the scientific method to delve into this question.

1. Ask a question
2. Research the topic of the question
3. Form a hypothesis about the question
4. Make a plan to test the hypothesis
5. Carry out the plan
6. Collect and Analyze data
7. Draw a conclusion about your hypothesis based on the data.
8. Share what you found out.

The Beginning:
To start, you need a question. Your question will look like this:

How does _____ affect the growth of grass?

It's a simple question that could change the world. Can the stuff that you throw away really make a better world? Over the next few months, you'll bring together everything you're learning in school to find out. How hard you work will not only determine your grade, but may be the beginning of a brighter future for all. The journey begins today.

Appendix C: Procedure Rubric

Science Fair Procedure Rubric

	4 Exemplary	3 Proficient	2 Needs Improvement	1 Unsatisfactory
Controlling Variables	Exemplary attention paid to controlling non-essential variables.	Procedure contains steps insuring non-essential variable are controlled leaving only one independent variable.	Non-essential variables are controlled enough to get usable data, but some variables remain uncontrolled.	Procedure contains too few controls on non-essential variables. Results will not be reliable.
Specificity	Exemplary detail is included in the measurements and amounts. Experiment could be easily repeated.	Measurements and amounts are indicated so that the experiment could be repeated.	Some measurements or amounts are indicated. Experiment would be difficult to repeat.	Few measurements or amounts are indicated. Experiment would be difficult to repeat reliably.
Format	All criteria for 3 are present and procedure also uses appropriate scientific vocabulary.	Procedure is written with the following criteria: 1. Steps are numbered 2. Steps are written in complete sentences 3. Steps are written with proper grammar and spelling.	Two criteria from the "3" column are present.	One criteria from the "3" column is present.

Appendix D: Conclusion Directions

Science Fair
Conclusion

Directions:

It's time to draw conclusions based on the evidence you gathered during your Science Fair experiment. The conclusion paragraph will have three parts.

1. **Claim**: State whether or not the evidence supports or does not support your hypothesis (was your hypothesis correct or incorrect!)
2. **Evidence**: State the evidence that proves your claim. This should be the data that you gathered. You're evidence should include numeric data.
3. **Reasoning**: Explain why your evidence proves your claim. In other words, explain how your evidence proves your hypothesis was correct or incorrect.

Note:

If you cannot tell if your hypothesis is correct or incorrect, then state that as your claim. Then describe the evidence and explain why it does not support or refute your hypothesis.

Turning it in:

When you're done writing your conclusion, log into turnitin.com. Click on your science section and click on "Science Fair Conclusion." Upload your Google document.

How I will grade your conclusion:

I will use the rubric on the back of this page to grade your conclusion.

Appendix E: Conclusion Rubric

Science Fair Conclusion Rubric

	Exemplary (4 pts)	Proficient (3 pts)	Needs Improvement (2 pts)	Unsatisfactory (1 pt)	No Evidence (0 pts)
Scientific Claim	Clear scientifically accurate claim that answers the prompt concisely and thoroughly using correct grammar and punctuation.	Clear scientifically accurate claim that sufficiently answers the prompt.	Claim reveals partial understanding and includes both accurate and inaccurate details or omits important details.	No identifiable statement of claim tied correctly to the question.	No claim present.
Evidence	Evidence (data) is complete, clear, and accurate, relevant, and specific to the claim.	Accurate and sufficient evidence (data) for the claim.	Some accurate evidence (data) for the claim but it is not sufficient to support it OR the evidence provided contains both accurate and inaccurate statements.	Evidence is inaccurate.	No Evidence.
Scientific Reasoning	Explicit reasoning that completely links the evidence to the claim. Includes the scientific principle involved in the claim.	Clear and sufficient reasoning links the evidence to the claim.	Partial reasoning that links the evidence to the claim but the reasoning is not sufficient OR contains both appropriate reasoning and reasoning that does not link the evidence to the claim.	The reasoning is inaccurate.	No Reasoning.

Appendix F: Abstract Directions

Science Fair
Abstract

Directions: The abstract is a brief introduction to your experiment. It is the last thing you will write, but will be the first part of your Science Fair lab report. Your abstract should be one paragraph long. It will consist of five parts.

1. **Introduction**. In the introduction, you explain why you did your experiment. You should also describe the relevance your experiment has to the world. Why would others care about the experiment you conducted and your conclusions. It may not be obvious to the reader so you have to explain it to them. Describe how this research may impact them or change the way they live. You want to make the reader interested enough to continue reading the paper.
2. **Problem Statement.** Identify the hypothesis you investigated.
3. **Procedures**. Describe how you went through your investigation. In narrative form, take the reader through your procedure. Don't list every step and every material unless it's necessary to get your point across. You're summarizing your procedure not going into detail. Make sure to include the most important variable from your experiment.
4. **Results**. When you finally had your data, what did you find out? Was your hypothesis supported or refuted? Was the data inconclusive? Use specific numbers to justify your results. Do not be vague. You're data is your greatest tool to back up your results.
5. **Conclusions**. Explain how your project contributes to our topic of making the world a better place through trash. Did you discover what you had hoped? What new research might you do

to continue your experiment or what new questions did your experiment lead to?

For your conclusions, if you did not get sufficient evidence and your results were inconclusive, reflect on what went wrong and how you would redesign your experiment differently.

Turning it in: When you're done with the Abstract, log onto turnitin.com and upload it.

Your Grade: I will grade your abstract using the rubric on the back.

Appendix G: Abstract Rubric

Science Fair Abstract Rubric

	3 Proficient	2 Needs Improvement	1 Unsatisfactory	Teacher Column
Completeness	All parts of the abstract are present.	The abstract is missing one or two parts.	Abstract lacks more than two parts of the summary.	What's Missing: __Intro __Problem __Procedure __Results __Conclusions
Accuracy	All parts of the Abstract accurately reflect the events and findings of the science fair experiment.	Most pars of the Abstract accurately reflect the events and findings of the science fair experiment.	Few parts of the Abstract accurately reflect the events and findings of the science fair experiment.	
Organization	Abstract has all parts organized in the correct order and the language is easy to read and follow.	Most Abstract parts are organized in the correct order. A small portion may be difficult to read and follow.	Abstract parts are not organized in the correct order or are difficult to follow.	
Grammar	There are no errors in spelling, punctuation or grammar.	There are one or two errors in spelling, punctuation or grammar.	There are more than two errors in spelling punctuation or grammar.	

Appendix H: Final Report Directions

Science Fair
Final Report

Directions: For this assignment, you will assemble all the pieces of your interdisciplinary Science Fair project that you completed in your various classes into one report. This report will represent all of your efforts to complete your experiment. The report will be in the form of a Google document that you will upload to turnitin.com. It will consist of the following parts. Each part will be a major heading in your paper.

Title Page:
On the title page, you will write a title for your project. Your title should be 10 words or less and should tell the reader what the experiment was about. Many students use their question as their title. The title should be in large font (around 30 pt.). Underneath the title, you should write your Latin subtitle/motto. You did this work in Latin class.

Page 1: Abstract
This will serve as an introduction to your report. You completed this in Science class. You will copy and paste it into your final report.

Page 2: Question
This was the original science research question. It was completed in Science and written in your Science Fair Journal on the first page.

Page 2: Background Research
This is the library/internet research that you did in Humanities class. You will also copy this into your final report.

Page 2. Hypothesis
This was your prediction that you made about the science research question based on the research you did. It was completed in Science and written in your Science Fair notebook. You will copy it into your final report.

Page 3: Materials and Procedure
You wrote these as a Google document as well as in your Science

Fair Journal in Science class. You will copy them into your final report.

Page 4: Data and results
This represents the graph you made in Math class. Your graph should be copied into your final report.

Page 5: Conclusion
This conclusion was written in Science class as a Google document. It represents what you learned by doing your Science Fair project. You will copy and paste it into your final report.

Page 6: Sources
On this page, you will list the internet and library sources you used to do your experiment. If you included information from your ELA reading, you need to include that source in your Sources Page as well. Use the sourcing method you use in Humanities.

Turning it in:
When you're done assembling all the parts of the Final Report, log into turnitin.com and upload the report.

Assessment:
There are nine parts to your final report. Each part is worth one point for a total of nine points. You will lose a point for each part your report is missing.

Appendix I: Visual Presentation Directions

Science Fair
Google Presentation

Introduction: You will be presenting your Science Fair Experiment to the class next week. You will make a **Google presentation** to accompany your oral presentation. Your presentation will be a summary of your whole experiment. It will have the following parts.

1. Your variable.
- Explain what your independent variable is and why you chose it.
- Provide any other information you can about your variable.

2. Your Hypothesis
- State your hypothesis
- Explain your reasons for your hypothesis.
- Use your <u>research</u> that you did in Humanities in your explanation.

3. Your experimental design
- This is a summary of how you set up your experiment.
- It should include not only how you set up the experiment, but also how you went about making measurements.
- It should include the details of your procedure that might make it different from the other teams' experiments.

4. The results
- Your data.
- Show your graph and explain it.

5. Your conclusion
- Explain if your hypothesis was supported by the evidence or not.
- Explain **how** the evidence does or does not support your hypothesis.

6. Reflection
- If your data did not allow you to draw a conclusion, explain why were you unable to draw a conclusion.
- Whether or not you were able to draw a conclusion, describe how you would improve your experimental design to get more informative results/data?
- Put your experiment into real world context. Explain how your experiment could be used in the real world. Who might find it useful? What for? You should use your independent reading

book from Language Arts to help you address these questions.
- Based on how you conducted your experiment and how it turned out, what other experiments might you do to extend your project and make it more useful?

7. When you are done...
- Change the name of the file to "sec# Team# Presentation." Then "share" the document with me.

How I will grade your presentation.

1. Every student in your group must participate meaningfully.
2. Each student will be graded individually on the presentation based on the whole school verbal communication rubric on the back of this paper.
3. Each student may receive a different grade depending on their level of participation and the quality of their part of the presentation.
4. Your team will have a total of five minutes to make the presentation.

Presentation Tips

1. Use what you know about oral presentations that you've learned from your other classes.
2. To make a Google presentation, go to your Google drive, click on "create." Then click on "presentation." The rest works very much like Power Point and Prezi. Don't put too much info on each slide. Less is more.
3. Spend no time on making it look fancy. Focus on the information. Time is short.
4. Use index cards to make a script for what each person will say during their part of the presentation.
5. Make sure everyone has an equal part. You will have a maximum of 5 minutes. If each person speaks for about a minute, you will not go over your time.

Appendix J: Oral Presentation Directions

Science Fair
Oral Presentation

Introduction: You will create a short oral presentation to go along with your Google Presentation. It will be a maximum of 5 minutes long. The oral presentation should be a summary of your whole experiment. It should give the viewers a very good idea of the process you went through, what you did, and what you found out. Every member of your team is expected to participate equally. Each member will receive an individual grade based on the amount of your participation and the quality of your participation. I will use the **whole school verbal communication rubric** to grade your presentation. It's on the next page.

Tips on creating your presentation:
- **Make your presentation complete.** When your presentation is done, everyone should understand exactly what you were trying to find out, why you were doing it, what you did, how you did it, and how it all turned out. Include everything. You are the teacher!
- **Be detailed and clear**. Your Google presentation is just a brief summary. You must communicate the details out loud. Elaborate on all the points in your Google presentation. For example, talk about the details of your procedure that will allow people to understand what you did. Explain the data so that it's clear how your graph connects to what happened during your weeks of measuring. Add personal points such as things that surprised you or things you found interesting, puzzling, or disappointing.
- **Reflect**. The end of your presentation is an opportunity to think about how your experiment went and what it could lead to in the future. Sometimes scientists decide that more data should be collected and they have ideas about how to improve their

experiment to get more or better data. Sometimes scientists have ideas about how to expand their experiment to new topics. Sometimes, during the experiment, a scientist will have questions about what they are observing. These questions can be the source of a new experiment.

- **Contextualize your project.** Explain how your little experiment about grass fits in to our world. What effect could it have on the world? Who might find your project important? Why? Use your Language Arts independent reading in your reflection.

Tips on giving your presentation:

- **Don't read the screen.** This is the biggest mistake people make when giving Science Fair oral presentations. They just read the information on the Google presentation slides. You need to tell all the details out loud. The slides are just a short summary. You may REFER to the slides, but do NOT simply read them out loud.
- **Don't read from your index cards.** This is the second biggest mistake people make when giving Science Fair oral presentations. Many students simply read the script off their cards. You may glance down at your cards to help remind you of what to say, but then you should look back up at the audience before you begin speaking.
- **Make eye contact.** Always look at the people listening to your presentation. You are talking to them. You are not talking to your index cards, the computer screen, or the floor, so don't look at those things when you're speaking.
- **Speak loudly.** Make sure the person in the back can hear you.

Appendix K: Presentation Rubric

Science Fair Presentation Rubric* (This is the Whole School Verbal Communication Rubric)

	4. Exemplary	3. Proficient	2. Needs Improvement	1. Unsatisfactory
Organization	Presentation has a clear beginning, middle and end and includes smooth transitions. The presenter clearly meets the objective of the assignment and expertly and consistently communicates the focused purpose.	Presentation has a clear beginning, middle and end. Transitions are present. The presenter meets the objective of the assignment and communicates purpose.	The beginning, middle and end of the presentation are unclear and transitions are infrequent or not smooth.	The presentation does not contain a beginning, middle or end and transitions are not indicated. The presenter does not clearly meet the objective of the assignment and does not communicate purpose.
Delivery	The presenter consistently engages the audience with an audible, clear voice using appropriate intonation, eye contact and appropriate body language. The presenter expertly adapts pace for effect and utilizes the allotted time effectively.	The presenter engages the audience with an audible, clear voice using appropriate intonation, some eye contact and appropriate body language. The presenter adapts pace for and utilizes the allotted time effectively.	The presenter attempts to engage the audience with an audible clear voice using appropriate intonation, infrequent eye contact and body language is not fully appropriate for the purpose. The presenter attempts to adapt pace for effect and utilizes most of the allotted time.	The presenter does not engage the audience with an audible, clear voice, has no eye contact and their body language is not appropriate for the purpose. The presenter does not adapt the pace for effect and ineffectively utilizes the allotted time.
Relevance	The presentation is complete, clear and accurate. The information is relevant and specific to the purpose and the evidence is utilized to support the argument. (e.g. step-by-step procedures, diagrams, graphs, etc.)	The presentation is complete, clear and accurate. Most information is relevant and specific to the purpose and most evidence is utilized to support the argument.	The presentation is complete, clear and accurate. Some information is relevant and specific to the purpose and some evidence is utilized to support the argument.	The presentation is not complete, clear and accurate. The information is not relevant nor specific to the purpose and no evidence is utilized to support the argument.

*This Rubric was developed by Boston Latin Academy and used to assess both the visual and oral presentation.

Appendix L: Student Evaluation Form

I made copies of the grid below for students to evaluate each team as they made their oral presentation to the class. The sheet I gave the students was two sided and had four of the grids on the front and four on the back. So, they could do eight evaluations. My classes are divided into seven teams of four students. Thus, they had plenty of grids to evaluate all the teams plus one extra in case they needed to discard one due to errors.

I collected the evaluation sheets at the end of class and gave students a completion grade for that day's classwork.

	No Evidence	Some Evidence	Clearly Evident
Eye Contact	0	1	2
Clearly Audible (loud enough)	0	1	2
Clearly explains Question & Hypothesis	0	1	2
Clearly and thoroughly explains experimental procedure	0	1	2
Clearly explains the data and how it helps prove or disprove the hypothesis.	0	1	2

Appendix M: Latin

Throughout this book, I've mentioned the interdisciplinary nature of our seventh grade Science Fair. I even teased that we made a connection to Latin class. It was a simple connection, but ended up being really cool.

Students had done independent reading in their Language Arts classes that helped them contextualize their grass experiment into a larger picture. The array of books selected by their LA teachers focused on food and environmental issues.

Near the end of the project when most of the work was done, the Latin teacher had students brainstorm a subtitle or motto for their project. They then translated the motto into Latin and it went on the cover of their final report.

This assignment allowed students to infuse a bit of creativity into what are normally pretty dry report titles. They had subtitles like "Saving the World One Blade at a Time." The subtitle was in Latin, of course.

The connection helped students think more about their small experiment in a big picture kind of way. In my experiences with traditional Science Fair, students struggle to connect their work with relevant real world issues. This Latin assignment, in conjunction with other work they'd done, gave them an opportunity to do just that.

Resources

Visit **www.sciencenugget.com/resources** to access PDF and MS Word versions of the resources in the appendices of this book. You can visit **http://tinyurl.com/mbuha2u** to go to a shared Google drive with a series of files in it. Both web locations include the directions and rubrics from the appendices, and other resources.

I've visited **sciencebuddies.org** frequently over the years for ideas and guidance when I've been stuck. They're organized around "old school" Science Fair. However, they have good suggestions for directions and rubrics.

Students in my classes created Google documents for most of their work. It allowed them to save their efforts in the cloud and avoid issues with lost papers, software compatibility, etc. Moreover, they can "share" their documents with each other and with me for feedback and support. They can also revert to previous versions of their work if it gets erased or otherwise unintentionally manipulated. Students can create Google documents in their Google drive once they've created a Gmail account. See **gmail.com** for more info.

I use **turnitin.com** for most of the work the students completed. It allows students to submit their work to me in one central location. They can upload their Google documents right to the web site. There is a rubric function that also makes assessing the work much easier. Finally, when all is said and done, you have a complete record of all the students' work archived. You can use this for exemplars in future years and for integrating Science Fair in your school vertically (up and down grade levels).

Rather than make tri-fold boards, I had students create Google presentations. This saved tons of paper and space in my classroom. Moreover it gave students an introduction to cloud collaboration, an important twenty first century skill. Students can create Google presentations in their Google drive once they've created a Gmail account. See gmail.com for more info.

Materials: The materials for this experiment were fairly inexpensive. I collected one dollar from each student and was able to purchase lab notebooks, soil, seed sprouters, sprouter trays, seeds, and pipettes. Here are some on-line sources for materials:

- Winter rye grass seeds. I use "Johnathan Green Winter Rye Grass Seed." A five pound bag from **Amazon.com** is enough to last a lifetime.
- Blue exam books to use as Science Fair notebooks. The "School Smart Ruled Examination Blue Books" came in a pack of one hundred and costs thirty bucks on **Amazon.com** as of this writing.
- Six pack seed sprouter. Search "seedling starter trays" on **Amazon.com** for plenty of inexpensive options.
- Containers for the sprouters. Search "growing trays" for a list. Double check to make sure the dimensions match the sprouters you buy.
- Pipettes. Some have milliliter graduations for easier measurement. The "Karter Scientific 206H2 3ml Grad Transfer Pipettes" come in a pack of 500. Enough for a lifetime for ten dollars on **Amazon.com**.

If you enjoyed this book, it would help me incredibly
if you left a review on **Amazon.com** or
another vendor site.

Sign up for my newsletter
to get updates on new books
and other resources:
sciencenugget.com/newsletter

Also, listen to my podcast
to hear how Science Fair plays out
in my classroom each day.
"The Science Fair Podcast" is on iTunes or Stitcher.

iTunes: **itunes.apple.com/us/podcast/the-science-fair-podcast/
id929626932**
Stitcher: **stitcher.com/s?fid=55748&refid=stpr**

For more info go to my website **sciencenugget.com**

About the Author

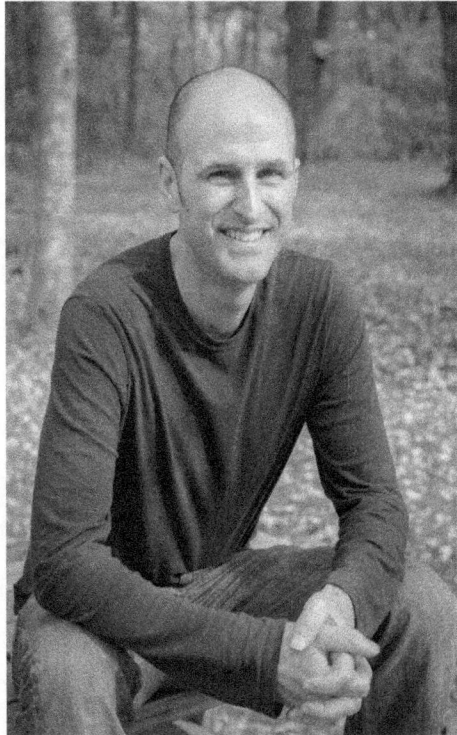

Adam Shopis is a thirteen year veteran middle school teacher. He has taught in the public schools in Boston Massachusetts for his entire career. During this time he has designed and conducted teacher training workshops for the city's sixth grade curriculum as well as rewritten a portion of that curriculum. For most of that time he'd suffered through Science Fair year after year, until he'd had enough and wrote this book. He lives in Boston with his wife and two sons. In the summertime he can be found waiting for waves on various breaks throughout New England.